—HOW—
CAN I LAUGH WHEN NOTHING'S FUNNY

Understanding and Overcoming

DEPRESSION

CRYSTAL SCOTT-LINDSEY,
LMFT, M.A., B.S.

authorHOUSE®

AuthorHouse™
1663 Liberty Drive
Bloomington, IN 47403
www.authorhouse.com
Phone: 1 (800) 839-8640

Published by AuthorHouse 08/21/2018

ISBN: 978-1-5462-5491-1 (sc)
ISBN: 978-1-5462-5490-4 (e)

Print information available on the last page.

CONTENTS

PREFACE

When I consider depression and human experiences, I think of the experience of an air mattress. Think and imagine with me for a moment. Humans are the air mattress and the pump that controls air in and air out represents the whole of our life experiences. On the air pump is a function that blows air in and the same pump has another function that sucks air out to flatten the air mattress conveniently. The same pump is responsible to give the mattress what it needs to be enjoyed and utilized, but when the pump is not used correctly, you can end up sucking air out of the mattress when you actually need air going into the mattress. Same pump, different experience.

Life is much like this at times. Experiences, relationships, our self, and so on, can prove to be avenues by which our world is filled with glee and bliss. However, these same avenues can also suck and drain the very life from us. When aspects of our life are not understood and handled properly, we can end up with unfavorable results from the exact same things in life that once yielded favorable results.

Consequently, more often than not, depression will be experienced.

Due to the sensitivity and oftentimes severity of the nature of individuals' concerns, before I sit with people to provide therapy, I keep in mind to meditate and pray for guidance and direction to be accurate and appropriate, to be in-tune, fully present and professional; yet human, approachable, and reachable. I give due diligence to viewing each person as unique and avoid cookie-cutter approaches, so that each person might get the most out of the therapeutic experience.

I have carefully selected the title of this book by asking a very poignant question: How Can I Laugh When Nothing's Funny? This is a valid question, because it can seem to be an arduous task to muster up a laugh when depressed. I then added a subtitle to suggest that, within the context and framework of this book, you will discover how to laugh again. I am honored to utilize my ways, words, grit, commitment, skillfulness, and ability to wield a wealth of knowledge, understanding, compassion, and care concerning each life I encounter. Sit back and relax, as you are introduced to my story.

My Story

It is befitting for me to begin by providing a cursory view of my experience with situational depression. Along my life journey I have interfaced with many challenges, some good and some not so good. There were times when such experiences rendered me depressed. As I aged and matured in life experiences I learned to accept that feeling depressed in certain moments in time; or being in a depressed state or mood (over a period of time) is not something to feel badly about or be ashamed of.

When my very first experience of depression happened, I did not know what it was. Perhaps I had experienced depression early in life and was not aware. For sure, I was depressed in my early 20s; I lost a sibling to murder. One would suspect that this could traumatize and depress anyone, but I did not think in terms of being depressed. I was angry for sure; but in retrospect, I was also depressed. Anger was a manifestation of my depression. I isolated from family and friends. Looking back, when I did engage with others it was all surface. I did not have the mental or emotional health to engage with any real happiness, laughter, depth or significant substance.

My depressive state lasted for a couple of years, but I did not know this at the time. I now know this was the case because when my grief and depression lifted, I was a much different, better person. I was much happier, more goal focused and creative. I found hope again and wanted to live life to the fullest. And then, my father passed away, and then my step-father passed away, and then I lost my spouse to a car accident. A year after that my dog I had for 14 years died in my arms. Yes, I know the heaviness, the pain, and the debilitating nature of depression all too well. I understand the grip of grief and the excruciating longing that takes over every part of your being at times. But I also know the joyful part of the aftermath. The period after grief and loss when I realized I was not destroyed. The moment when I awakened to a new lease on life, if-you-will.

Now I will share with you a couple of areas I became really stuck in, as related to depression associated with grief and loss. First, I will describe the events related to the death of my step-father, who was an amazing man in so many ways. When I learned that he had been diagnosed with cancer I chose to believe he would be miraculously healed. As time went on the reports became more and more grim. When it seemed as if things would not take a turn for the better I knew I had to fly in to see him sooner rather than later. Now, for my challenge. The day before I was scheduled to fly out and see him he passed away. I got stuck in the anger and bargaining phase of grief and loss, and depression because I stated and restated: "only if I had gone sooner." Of course, I blamed myself. I was so angry and thought, had I only tried harder I would have been able to say goodbye. I had not seen him for 3 years prior, and I never saw him alive again.

My dog presented another challenge. He died in my arms. I don't remember ever feeling as helpless as I felt in that moment. I did not realize that each whimper and whine was him slowly dying. I held him in desperation and believed with all my heart that my love and prayer for him would be strong enough to keep him alive; but he died. At that very moment I felt so utterly and completely alone. I felt like I failed him somehow. Then of course, all the past hurts from all of my other losses came rushing in. The wave of grief took over me. I became angry and resentful. The heaviness and the weight of grief sat on me like a ton of bricks. In my imagination, coming out of this state seemed synonymous to taking on the challenge of single-handedly moving the greatest mountain. I do not remember ever feeling quite so alone.

You see, my dog (scooter) was like losing a best friend:

like a family member for sure. He was there through the raising of my 2 children, the loss of my father and step-father, my undergraduate and graduate studies, my relocation and transition from the west coast, and the loss of my spouse. At some point, I cannot pinpoint when, I began to feel my healing and my strength resurface, I then wrote this declaration:

Stripped and Amazed

I stand stripped, vulnerable, and transparent.
Stripped of all defenses as God's peace floods my
soul. With amazing and incomprehensible
grace I am able to stand strong. I am empowered
as I take in the magnitude of the love of God
that is shown to me. Without faith my very foundation
would be terribly shaken and I would not be able to stand
I am an awe-struck, reverent, and trembling
soul. Not trembling in fear, but in
amazement at how far I have come and how
much farther I know I can continue on.

So, my motivation to speak on depression runs deeper than research and textbook knowledge. There is a personal, driving bent or slant to my motivation, a force that motivates me to encourage you. Feeling sad and depressed is a part of life. As thinking, feeling, emoting, and behaving beings, difficulties of life will impact. How quickly one recovers is determined by many factors including but not limited to personality, ability to cope and manage life, support systems, and much, much more.

Additionally, willingness to let others in to share the load when you are feeling down and sad can play a major role in whether or not you get the help you need sooner rather than later. There might be times when you feel depressed and you hide behind a façade of happiness. Perhaps you go along to get along. If this is you, others might not be able to see pass your façade. You might come across as having it all together and that you are able to manage life's difficulties. Maybe you have been doing a good job without any need for much support, help or intervention thus far; but maybe there are times when you are actually wearing a mask; you might be depressed and unable to go through it alone. Indulge me as I share a portion of one of my favorite readings that depict this claim. Edwin Arlington pens a poem:

Richard Cory
Whenever Richard Cory went downtown,
We people on the pavement looked at him:
And Richard Cory, one calm summer night,
Went home and put a bullet through his head.

Looks can be deceiving. In this poem, Richard Cory was someone to be admired and it seemed he had it all together. According to the poem, some were even jealous. As you have read and probably have experienced with self and/or others, cues and signs can be missed. It is never a good idea to assume everyone is alright just by their outward presentation.

Those who are depressed, looking at someone who appears to have no reason to be depressed might even be a little envious. Just because some individuals might have no financial issues, no relationship issues, no health issues; this does not mean that these same individuals are impervious to depression. Depression can be experienced by the rich and the poor, the famous and the unknown, the loner and the life of the party: no one is untouchable when it comes to depression.

Just consider cakes for example. There are certain ingredients that are common to cakes in general. When baking a cake from scratch, you might commonly use ingredients such as eggs, milk or water. You might also use oil or butter, vanilla, baking powder, sugar, and so on. These are what I would call core, common ingredients. That which separates kinds of cakes is the type and flavor. Such as coconut, chocolate, vanilla, lemon, strawberry, banana, etc. Regardless, we will identify each as cake; and for sure all these flavors share the majority of common ingredients.

Human beings are not much different. We are common at our core. Our biological, psychological, and emotional makeup goes through the same growth processes. We are healthy versus unhealthy, in these realms, depending on other variables we encounter that might not be similar. Our experiences in life and how we respond makes us distinct, much like the cake example I described previously. All-in-all, we are all vulnerable to experiences that can lead to depressive symptoms. No one escapes. Whether the range of depressive symptoms are mild to extreme, no one escapes.

INTRODUCTION

Within the same timeframe of developing this manuscript, I see a headline flash across my computer screen. On February 1, 2018, Fidel Castro's son (Diaz-Balart, also known as Fidelito) commits suicide after battling depression. He had a history of being treated for depression through inpatient and outpatient services. A few other well-known individuals have recently committed suicide. Additionally, Michelle Williams, former singer with Destiny's Child disclosed her challenge to overcome depression.

Overwhelming evidence and statistical data supports what I cannot deny or ignore: the ever-increasing percentage of depressed women, men, children, and teens. This book will not provide statistical data specifically; however, this book is compiled utilizing sample experiences of my work as a therapist over-time, as well as empirical and academic data as related to depression. Resources and recommended readings are provided to further your knowledge and understanding as well. So, let's take a cursory look at how depression is described.

Depression is described as a debilitating disease,

characterized by despondency and despair, and if severe enough it can immobilize every part of your being. Depression can cause impairment in many areas of life such as emotions, mentality, spirituality, finances, relationships, and the workplace. Have you seen commercials advertising for antidepressant medication? There are quite a few out there. One that stands out for me demonstrates quite accurately how depressed individuals sometimes wear the mask of a smile or laughter, but deep down inside they are hiding their depression. In this commercial, individuals carry around a picture of a smile and the picture is held up over the face, to illustrate how some people get through life pretending that they are amused or merry, when; in fact, they are not. This brings to mind a snippet of a poem I learned in school a while back: We Wear the Mask by Paul Laurence Dunbar:

We wear the mask that grins and lies…
It hides our cheeks and shades our eyes…
But let the world dream otherwise…
We wear the mask!

Over the course of my professional and personal life I have had this statement told to me: "I know some people who mask depression very well." Perhaps you have also heard this statement a time or two as well. Of course, not all depressed individuals are somber and withdrawn in their behavior or manifestation of their depression. A radio DJ addressed the issue of the depression and she stated: "check on your strong friends." I get it. It makes sense. Some of the strongest presentations we see and experience might be those who are most likely masking depression.

Just think with me for a moment. You might recall comedians such as Chris Farley and Robin Williams. These two stand out for me for sure because I would not have thought they were depressed. But of course, I only saw them when they were in their comedic element. Perhaps those close to them knew and saw some signs, or maybe not. Yet, they kept at comedy and this is true for others we know. Hiding behind joking and pseudo-happiness is sometimes a coping mechanism. There are times when people are able to convincingly fake it until they are not able to hide depression any longer.

Life is difficult and challenging at times, no doubt, and along with difficult and challenging times, depressed individuals oftentimes do not want to be transparent, for good reasons I am sure. There are times when it seems no one cares and if someone does care, the question arises: what can anyone do? As a result, a sense of hopelessness ensues. When depression is experienced, this does not necessarily mean someone is experiencing a chemical imbalance resulting in depression. There is such a thing as situational depression and other reasons why someone might feel depressed due to circumstances and situations. During my graduate studies, one of my professors (Hank) told me to use this strategy to determine if someone is situationally or circumstantially depressed.

Hank said it in this manner: "when you are working with a depressed person, ask the miracle question." He said ask the patient if he or she woke up tomorrow and would be able to make any request, what would it be and would it be exciting. Hank then proceeded to say, if the patient cannot imagine any difference that might improve or lift the mood of depression, the patient is probably chemically depressed, because the patient cannot imagine a more pleasurable situation that could lift the mood. This could mean a chemical imbalance in the brain is happening for one reason or another. I have tried this query with patients, and it serves as grist for the mill when diagnosing and developing an accurate treatment plan. This is not a hard and fast way of accurately diagnosing, this is a tool to add along with other professional diagnostic tools.

Other variables are worth evaluating and considering to arrive at an appropriate diagnosis, but this simple tool is one way to get closer to a more accurate diagnosis, by attempting to tap into whether or not a depressed mood is more about what a person is experiencing externally (situationally), and possibly temporarily versus what that person is experiencing inwardly, or biochemically as well. Because depression involves self-reporting, it can also be helpful to see a medical doctor who might be able to perform tests such as lab work to determine if other deficiencies might be contributing to depression.

In this book you will learn how to understand your mind and body, and how they work in tandem, letting you know if you might be experiencing depression; or perhaps you might know of someone you think could be dealing with depression, and you can be a source of direction for those who could benefit from this reading. You will also have an opportunity to gain insight regarding the interconnectivity of the brain, mind, emotions and body as related to depression. Finally, you will receive information on helpful tips of dealing with depression, statistical data, and much more. While I am aware that depression has been around for a long time, and there is much that has been discussed and taught on this subject; I am prompted to write and share because there is a rise in the number of depressed individuals across gender, culture, socioeconomic status, and generations.

What the world is facing today is an epidemic of hopelessness resulting in self-injury or self-harming behavior, and suicide. When I speak of self-harm, I am not limiting this idea to self-mutilation. I am also referring to risk taking behaviors such as excessive use of drugs and alcohol to cope. I am also referring to indiscriminately engaging in sexual behaviors to feel better, that can result in incurable and sometimes deadly diseases.

Invariably, when someone is in emotional distress and feeling depressed, the goal is to feel better. When individuals do not possess the cognitive ability to think and problem solve effectively, and when there is a challenge to implement emotional intelligence, it can be very difficult to think and imagine that things can change. When individuals are steeped in and flooded with overwhelming emotions and thoughts associated with depression there is NO ability to think themselves into a better place without help. This help might be sufficiently found through psychotherapy, but there are times when symptoms are so severe that medication as an adjunct service, and perhaps hospitalization might be necessary to keep such individuals from spiraling downward to a very deep, dark place, and possibly becoming suicidal.

Throughout this reading I am going to stress the correlation between depression and suicidality because in the past year alone I have interfaced with many attempted and completed suicides. After the fact, most people acquainted with such individuals stated that they did not see it coming. My goal is to increase insight and heighten awareness that there can be severe effects and consequences when depression is left unattended.

I have not read many books on depression, with humor added to the context. Depression is generally discussed with seriousness because depression is a very serious matter; however, depression is not a death sentence. My desire is that you will arrive at a point of understanding and embracing a new thought about depression, as you learn about depression in a way that places you in a more powerful position over depression. This book is designed and intended to get you to a place of gaining mastery over possible fears and angst when you think about depression, and to teach you how to laugh again.

As you engage in this reading, you are sure to be reacquainted with some information you have already learned; and I am confident that you will also learn new insights. Allow this material to serve as a guide to greater understanding as related to your experience with depression. Also, be sure to practice mindfulness of those around you. Now that you have this reading in your possession, you might be surprised that maybe you have missed some subtle signs and red flags. In fact, you might also be surprised that depression is all around you, and possibly within you, more than you have realized.

Sadness is a normal emotion to have... overwhelming, relentless sadness can lead to depression.

CHAPTER 1

RECOGNIZING DEPRESSION

Have you ever been standing at the corner of "oh, come on!" and what the heck is going on? It is that place where turning around is useless, and you do not know what is ahead of you; so, you just stand. Immobilized and paralyzed in your thoughts and emotions. You are unsure what to do. You can see this moment as a place of transition or a place of stuckness that you cannot see your way out of. The more you see no way out; that is, the more hopeless you become, the more depressed you become.

I have been here before, experiencing times that have caused me to cry out in a tearful outburst because of disbelief that "this thing is happening to me!" In recognizing that depression can be a response to unfavorable circumstances,

I learned that feeling depressed is nothing to be ashamed of; it is actually a part of life. Once I allowed myself to accept the fact that depressing moments will be experienced, I went to work on managing my thoughts to minimize the possibilities of depressive symptoms looming and taking control of my life.

The following poem is an expression of what a person might experience when feeling depressed:

You want to laugh but you feel the cry,
Pressing on your heart consuming every part.
You do your best to fight back the tears,
and the all-consuming fears.
It's like a dagger that pierces and the pain is fierce,
You want to stay strong but find it difficult to go on.
You withdraw, hoping no one would ever know it,
The pain and the shame that permeates
every fiber of your being
You feel like you are losing it and the only option is to quit.
You reason with yourself that perhaps everyone
would be better off without you,
And giving up is the only imaginable thing to do.
It's not that you don't want things to change,
But you've grown hopeless because each day
you awaken things remain the same.
Hopelessness has you in a chokehold,
suffocating you to the core,
Until in anguish you cry out, no more.
Everyone tells you it will get better someday,
But the mental and emotional pain never goes away.

It's like a tether, you feel bound and oppressed;
you want the agony to cease,
So that you can finally, finally feel some relief.

What does depression look like? If you think in terms of being able to recognize it in every depressed person you are absolutely incorrect. Some people are very astute at masking what is going on. In fact, some people might go a lifetime and live with depression untreated. These would be the individuals who are simply good at pretending. This is a learned behavior. The one problem with pretending is this: when people go about with their lives as if everything is okay and these individuals are truly depressed, they might live a lifetime; but they will have lived a lifetime without living up to their full potential or capacity. I say this because depression is a thief. It robs and steals, and takes away from life that could and would otherwise be enjoyed.

Some ways of identifying depression

When depressed you might experience the following:

Feeling hollow or empty
A feeling of nothingness, feeling void, meaningless, and unfulfilled. These feelings can be in relation to self, others, things, and one's own usefulness in the world.

Sadness
Down, heartbroken, feeling of misery and maybe even feeling heaviness and a weightiness that is similar to grieving when someone dies.

Alone

A sense that no one else is around, even in a crowd. The feeling of aloneness not only speaks of being alone in the sense of an absence of people, but being alone in one's own pain, as if no one else can relate or has ever felt your level of pain, aloneness, and emptiness.

Afraid

Fear of the unknown and especially afraid you will not be able to figure or find a way to a happier you.

Angry

An intense emotional experience of dissatisfaction and vexation, as if an injustice has been done against you. Something is happening that should not be happening.

Agitated

A physical experience of being nervous and physically unable to calm down.

Irritable

Irritability is usually confused with agitation, but being irritable is more of a temperament. Being irritable is synonymous to being grumpy, crabby, difficult to please, touchy, and cranky.

Hopeless

Being hopeless suggests that you cannot see how things will ever change. Thinking that your situation will always be what it is or perhaps even worsen.

You might demonstrate:

Isolative behavior

Isolative behavior is when you begin to disconnect from relationships you once enjoyed. This might also include frequent absenteeism from work or school.

Suicidal thoughts

Thinking and pondering about what it would be like to no longer be alive to deal with the hopelessness and emotional pain. Perhaps even putting a plan in place.

Risk taking behaviors

Risk taking behaviors can include beginning to depend on drugs, prescriptions, and alcohol to cope. Also, making poor decisions as related to finances, legal issues, road raging, and indiscriminate sexual encounters.

Difficulty getting along with others

Increased arguments at home, work, and school, sometimes escalating to physical confrontation. Decreased respect for authority and others around you in general.

Staying busy

Staying busy goes along with the agitated person who cannot seem to calm down physically. Staying keyed up and raring to go. Looks a lot like anxiety, but can be a manifestation of agitated depression.

Men and Depression: a cursory overview

There are times when it is very difficult to get some male patients to use the word depressed, or some other more vulnerable words like sad, hurt, afraid, and lonely. And then there are other male patients who are very much in touch with their emotions and do not mind at all speaking candidly about being vulnerable and depressed. I generally go at each person's pace until there is comfortability with talking about depression, if depression is what is truly experienced. After rapport and trust is developed, there are times when a male patient might say: I think I might be depressed. Again, I go at each person's pace. The real work with overcoming depression begins when denial is not present.

Additionally, there is such a thing as agitated depression; as I mentioned earlier. This is probably why men tend to be more comfortable with and will readily acknowledge that they are angry and agitated versus sad and hurt. Some men do not realize that depression is highly manifested in men by way of anger outbursts, road rage, risk taking behaviors, and extreme edginess, irritability, and agitation. I am aware that some men are very much in touch with their dudeness, their machismo if-you-will; and I respect each and every individual's unique position. At the end of the day, my goal is to educate and help individuals gain awareness of what is really being experienced; even when it is most difficult to talk about. This is when reliance on the therapeutic alignment and the patient-therapist trusting relationship gets me through such challenges with my patients. Finally, I remain abreast of current research and therapeutic resources to have patients to take home. Sometimes this is an easier way of conveying information that might permeate barriers that exist due to the difficulty of discussing depression.

Women and Depression: a cursory overview

In comparison to men, women tend be more expressive with softer, despondent emotions; and not so much aggressive, risky behavior as men. However, it is important to note that some women display signs of agitated depression just as men, and some men are as solemn, sad, and withdrawn as women. The manifestation of depressive symptoms solely depends on each individual; nonetheless, documented research reveals common differences between the way women and men display depressive symptoms.

Because depression is based on self-report of symptoms experienced over a period of time, what is reported is taken into consideration; and when the criteria is appropriately met a diagnosis is concluded. This process is good for quantitative as well as qualitative data. However, when addressing depressive issues in therapy, it is helpful for me to get to know the total person. Sure, understanding symptoms and timeframes, family history, and life experiences associated with depression are all helpful in providing care and best practice. However, what I consider rewarding is getting to know so much more about the person outside of the painful experiences.

Do not misunderstand, these factors are important for all of my patients. As patients open up, invariably I get to know issues and concerns about individuals that sometimes are not revealed right away. I have an opportunity to feel with them and I feel for them, and all at the same time I see amazing people sit before me who have been weighed down by life and relationships, weighed down by family issues, mistakes and bad decisions, regrets, resentments and setbacks; I see it all and I still feel hopeful. You see, it takes amazing strength and courage to sit with a complete stranger and bear your heart and soul, and share intimate, personal details of your life. I never take it for granted or take it lightly when someone selects me to share their life journey and their pain. I count it an honor and privilege and I endeavor to do due diligence each and every session.

As I stated a few sentences back, I have also worked with men who are equally as weighed down by life, depressed, and committed to the therapeutic process. The number of men pale in comparison to women, or at least for my caseload of course. But this in no way slights men and how they too deal with depression.

Children and Depression: a cursory overview

Children also display depressive symptoms emotionally, *cognitively, physically, and behaviorally.* Now, more than ever before, children are engaging in self-harming behaviors. When depressed some children become too clingy or too aloof, acting-out behaviors such as tantrums and outbursts, sex, alcohol, drugs, and other criminal behaviors might be displayed. Also, when depressed; some children will become withdrawn and escape to video games or an excessive amount of time might be spent on electronics. Physically there might be a change in appetite and weight, children might experience sleep issues as well. A decline in grades/academics, and/or loss of interest in school could also be experienced.

Finally, depressed children indicate symptoms by speaking language of low self-esteem: such as "I am not good enough, nobody likes me, I'm bad, and worst of all; I don't want to live anymore." These symptoms can be detected in children as young as 10 years old and under. Because depression is on the rise, the moment you see signs; reach out for help. It is always better to be on the safe side. So, you might be wondering; what can I do to help my child with depression? Aside from getting the child assessed, you can talk to your child. There are books to help your child get comfortable talking about depression. Age does matter, and the child's level of understanding of terms and what is being experienced emotionally and mentally matters. For starters try these strategies:

1. Don't allow the child to spend too much time alone
2. Don't overload the child with more than the child can handle. Sometimes pressure from overachievers can create depression and even anxiety in children
3. Talk about symptoms with the child in terms the child can understand
4. Help the child with a balanced life
5. Be sure there is no bullying going on with the child
6. Monitor the child's time alone with electronics and know what the child is entertaining on electronics
7. Stay in touch with teachers and coaches for feedback
8. Reach out to the child's pediatrician and a mental health professional

Teens and Depression: a cursory overview

According to The American Foundation of Suicide Prevention, suicide is the leading cause of death in teens in the United States. The teen developmental stage presents challenges that could lead to depressive symptoms. Central to the teen developmental stage, according to psychanalyst

Erik Erikson, is the task to master issues associated with physical maturation, peer and group relationships, and emotional development. Erikson identifies the age range of 12-18 for this period of development, and he suggests if challenges of development are mastered, what is learned is the ability to experience healthy relationships with peers and peer groups.

On the other hand, if mastery does not go well, the teen might experience isolating behaviors and feelings of detachment. Of course, other family, social, biological, and environmental factors certainly add to the mix of this particularly challenging time of development, such as parent-teen relationship issues that typically result from parents and teens not understanding each other. All such variables should be considered to understand how teens develop, to help teens deal with depressive symptoms, and to help them understand and recover.

Following, you will notice an outline of developmental stages that might help with understanding the big picture of development; and also help with connecting the dots of development throughout life. This is very important to know because mastery of each successive stage depends on mastery of each previous stage. If you already have my book; Communication and You, you will recognize this Stages of Development Chart.

STAGES OF DEVELOPMENT

Erik Erikson, a psychoanalyst, developed a psychosocial theory about human beings. According to Erikson, different developmental stages presents a different **psychological**

crisis to master and a **developmental task** to learn; additionally, a **central process** is experienced. When development goes well mastery is experienced and **ego quality** is healthy. When there is difficulty or unhealthy relationships are experienced, individuals might deal with maladjustment and **core pathological** issues. The following is a concise delineation of Erikson's stages of development:

Ages 0-2
Psychosocial Crisis: Basic trust versus mistrust
Ego Quality: Hope
Central Process: Mutuality with Caregiver
Developmental Task: Social attachment/ emotional development
Core Pathology: Withdrawal

Ages 2-3
Psychosocial Crisis: Autonomy versus shame and doubt
Ego Quality: Will
Central Process: Imitation
Developmental Task: Language development, self-control, fantasy play
Core Pathology: Compulsion

Ages 4-6
Psychosocial Crisis: Initiative versus guilt
Ego Quality: Purpose
Central Process: Identification
Developmental Task: Gender identification, moral development, self-theory, group play
Core Pathology: Inhibition

Ages 6-12
Psychosocial Crisis: Industry versus inferiority
Ego Quality: Competence
Central Process: Education
Developmental Task: Friendships, skill-learning, self-evaluation, and team play
Core Pathology: Inertia

Ages 12-18
Psychosocial Crisis: Group identity versus alienation
Ego Quality: Fidelity
Central Process: Peer pressure
Developmental Task: Physical maturation, sexual relations, peer groups, emotional development
Core Pathology: Dissociation

Ages 18-24
Psychosocial Crisis: Individual identity versus identity confusion
Ego Quality: Fidelity continued
Central Process: Role experimentation
Developmental Task: Autonomy from parents, career choices, internalized morality
Core Pathology: Repudiation

Ages 24-34
Psychosocial Crisis: Intimacy versus isolation
Ego Quality: Love
Central Process: Mutuality among peers
Developmental Task: Exploring intimate
relations, childbearing, work, lifestyle
Core Pathology: Exclusivity

Ages 34-60
Psychosocial Crisis: Generativity versus stagnation
Ego Quality: Care
Central Process: Person-environment fit, creativity
Developmental Task: Manage careers, nurture
intimate relationships, manage household
Core Pathology: Rejectivity

Ego Qualities Defined:

Hope= an enduring belief that one can attain one's own
deep and essential wishes

Will= a determination to exercise free choice and self-control

Purpose= the courage to imagine and pursue valued goals

Competence= the free exercise of skill and intelligence in
the completion of tasks

Fidelity= the ability to freely pledge and sustain loyalty to
others

Love= a capacity for mutuality that transcends childhood dependency

Care= a commitment to concern about what has been generated

Confidence= a conscious trust in oneself and assurance about the meaningfulness of life

Core Pathologies Defined:

Withdrawal= depression, isolation, detachment

Compulsion= a psychological and usually irrational force that makes somebody do something, often unwillingly

Inhibition= shyness, embarrassment, overly self-conscious

Inertia= lethargy, disinterest, inaction, sluggishness, indolence, unwillingness

Dissociation= detachment, separation, disconnection, severance, alienation, division

Repudiation= rejection, abandonment, refusal, disallowance

Exclusivity= excluding, or intending to exclude many from participation or consideration, conceited, pompous, showy, fake

Rejectivity= refuse to accept, agree to, believe in, or make use of something

A perpetual depth that consumes
every part of you—
A sunken place.

CHAPTER 2

A SUNKEN PLACE

Disappointment is generally associated with depression and can stem from unrealized hopes and expectations. A feeling of disappointment can be created by being let down by *self* and/or others. Consequently, if an experience is depressing; you become depressed. How long a depressed state lasts depends on your insight and ability to not allow disappointment to override what you know about *you* and your capabilities. You are so much more than what you did, or did not do, or could not do, or would not do. You are far more than your regrets, mishaps, and others' opinion of you. Your limitations define you only if you allow them to define you, so don't.

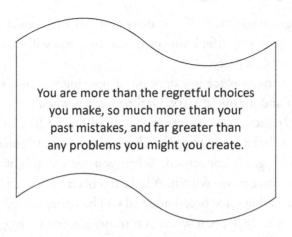

You are more than the regretful choices
you make, so much more than your
past mistakes, and far greater than
any problems you might you create.

Do not perpetuate a systemic thought-life that is non-productive. Rather, cultivate a mindset that is patient and gracious toward yourself. This does not mean that you are passive and blasé, nor does this mean that you are not driven and motivated to meet certain expectations for yourself. This means that you are realistic and you understand that everyone has limitations. When you have been let down by others, situations, or let down by yourself, regardless of the source; hit the reset button. Re-strategize and set realistic, attainable goals. Go back in with a fresh plan; fresh eyes, fresh ears, fresh ideas; and try again! In doing so, you can significantly decrease the chances that you will end up in a prolonged state of depression that leads to a sunken place.

It might come across to you that I am suggesting this is an easy thing to do. Of course not. I am fully aware that what I am stating is not easy. However, I am sharing with you much-needed hope and courage that can spark the notion to believe and hope again. Nothing worth attaining is *usually* easy, but ask yourself if it is worth it to you. The beauty of it all is that you get to decide. Because you are filled with great potential, if you deny yourself the opportunity to live your best life; I am concerned that you will sink to a dark, sunken place.

A sunken place is a dark pit of nothingness that sucks you in and drains you dry. Darkness exists when there is no light. In fact, darkness reveals a lack of light. Once light is present darkness disappears. This is also a true statement as far as insight is concerned. When you receive insight, this means you can see within. A light has been turned on. The darkness that once overshadowed you has disappeared. But this can only happen when you transition from struggling with darkness to striving toward the light.

Sure, when you deal with depression you are drained of your energy, time, talents, dreams, aspirations, and yes; you are drained of your very hope that things can possibly turn around. It can be difficult to resonate with or relate to this sunken place if you have never been there. Relating to someone's pain and the paralysis that this place creates cannot be imagined by some. Nonetheless, the sunken place of depression is real. The immobilization that accompanies this dark pit can overtake and overwhelm, and can leave one feeling isolated, afraid, and ashamed. There are some who are able to return from a sunken place, and sadly enough some do not; but there is hope as long as you are still alive, willing to strive, and have the necessary tools and support to get through your sunken place.

So how does one get to a sunken place during depression? When signs and symptoms of depression are not recognized readily and dealt with quickly and effectively, a sunken place is more likely to be experienced. Here are some possibilities of why individuals might experience difficulty recognizing signs of depression sooner, and as a result the likelihood of sinking into the dark, deep pit of despair is much greater. First, some people do not understand what depression really is. Some people think that life should be dealt with and if we are strong we can overcome difficulties without being overtaken by depression. In sum, for individuals in this category, being depressed is a no-no. Just pick yourself up, think better, and you will feel better. These are the things some people are actually told. Additionally, some individuals suppress their symptoms because life goes on and demands attention, so there is no time to deal with depression. But this causes a deeper level of sinking to the dark place. When you deal with depression in secrecy it festers.

Spiritually speaking, in times past; when individuals were depressed they were considered, by some, to be possessed with a demon. The remedy was to simply pray a little longer and harder, have more trust and faith in God, or change sinful lifestyles and habits to feel better. Additionally, culture can be a huge factor for some individuals, as it relates to depression. When there is a fundamental life desire or direction in life individuals would like to pursue, but such choices might be in opposition to what is culturally accepted, some people tend to experience depression. It depends on how closely tied individuals are to their culture.

Whether the source is individual, cultural, spiritual, relational, or a combination thereof; for sure, individuals are learning more and more about the reality of depression as a disease and the danger of not taking precautions sooner rather than later. People are more accepting of the fact that many factors, beyond individuals' control, can contribute to depression. Secondly, there are some who are aware of their bout with depression; but are trying dealing with their depression alone, thinking it will just get better over time. Thirdly, there are those who reach out for help; but they do not stay the course or commit to treatment that is needed.

Sometimes treatment is long-term, sometimes it is long-term and multi-modality in nature. Multi-modality simply means that more than one method of treatment might be used, such as: therapy (family, group, and individual), psychiatric treatment (medication management), hospitalization or partial hospitalization program (PHP). For various reasons, there are some individuals who do not establish a commitment to the care that is necessary for their unique needs.

It takes amazing fight-back strength and a healthy, strong, supportive network to help you get through and out of a sunken place to which you have fallen, and to help you through your life recovery process. Of course, sometimes individuals are so deeply and severely depressed that medication or maybe hospitalization is necessary. Being accurately assessed and diagnosed is very important. If medication is utilized as an adjunct service, it is also important to be on the correct medication and dosage, being properly medicated and receiving ongoing therapy treatment could possibly determine the course of your recovery.

Let's Talk about Suicide and Depression

As difficult a topic suicide is, when someone actually commits suicide, they do so from a sunken place. This is not to suggest that everyone who experiences a sunken place will commit suicide. No, of course not. However, because a sunken place is such a dark, horrible pit that people cannot seem to think their way out of, the likelihood of suicidal ideation, suicide attempts, and suicide completions are greater.

So, how does one determine if feeling depressed is just a fleeting emotional experience that will pass, and nothing more serious? A depressive mood lasting for 2 consecutive weeks that includes the criteria outlined in the Diagnostic and Statistical Manual for Mental Illness (DSM 5) qualifies you for a depressive disorder:

1. Depressed mood most of the day
2. Loss of interest or pleasure most of the day
3. Change in weight or appetite (as significant as a 5% change)
4. Observe psychomotor (physical agitation) or rigidness
5. Fatigue
6. Feelings of guilt or worthlessness
7. Difficulty concentrating or making decisions
8. Insomnia or hypersomnia
9. Recurrent thoughts of death or suicide, or suicide attempts

Symptoms must cause significant impairment or distress, cannot be related to a substance or medical condition, there cannot be another diagnosis such as a psychotic disorder that might better explain such symptoms, and there has never been mania or a hypomanic episode.

At least 5 or more symptoms are required within 2 consecutive weeks. *DSM-5 American Psychiatric Association*

Treatment Approach

Cognitive Behavioral Therapy (CBT) is widely used for the treatment of depression. It is suggested that when you change your perspective you can change your mood, and then you can see your depression lift. However, one of the most difficult things for some humans to do is think outside of their own fixed idiosyncrasies and ways of understanding self, others, and the world. The more stuck you are in depression, the more difficult it can be to think differently, hopefully, and healthily.

As we grow and develop, we learn how to think about life in certain ways; we also learn how to attach meaning, feelings, and emotions to our experiences through relational frames. According to Dr. Richard Nongard, in his writing on Contextual Psychology, he states that "relational frames are the mental and often subconscious/unconscious constructs that support an idea, a belief, an experience, an interaction, or an action." The more we advance in age, the more we become more solid in our cognition and ways of being in the world. In this process, we find the difficulty that is faced when trying to think our way out of depression, out of a sunken place, and into a healthy mental and emotional state; but today this all can change. My challenge to you is this: Set yourself up for success by making profound changes. Will it be easy? I suppose not. Old habits tend to die hard.

Regardless, do not allow yourself to settle for less than you desire, even if somehow you have stopped believing that you can live depression-free. Get back in the fight.

As I am inputting this entry, I am reflecting on moments following the NFL playoff game between the New Orleans Saints and the Minnesota Vikings. Minnesota started out strong and from all appearances it looked like The Saints were not going to win. Eventually, The Saints caught up and took the lead, by the 4th quarter. If any of you reading this book also watched this game, you know it was a nail-biting and teeth gritting experience. For sure when there was less than 50 seconds left on the clock, in the 4th quarter; I was sure Minnesota was done. However, they did not give up. They did not let all that was against them stop them from visualizing the potential ahead of them.

With the information provided thus far, you might wonder—so Crystal, tell me: I still don't understand… how can I laugh? Let me begin by encouraging you to discover your *why*. Ask yourself why you should laugh, and this might lead you to your *how*. Here is another piece of information about me and depression. When I attended graduate school, during the last 2 years of my studies I concurrently started my internship. My internship professor was someone I highly respected. Students were asked to present cases during his class to be shared with others, have questions asked and answered, and receive feedback.

When it was my day to present, along with a couple of other students, I listened as others were commended on their work with patients. I anticipated receiving similar feedback. After my presentation, my professor did not have much to say. Not many questions were asked. However, when I received my paper back, my professor had written, in red, all the things that I could have and should have done differently. Now, maybe I was hypersensitive. I really did not know what was written on other students' paper; but his response let me feeling pretty icky. I questioned whether or not I was cut out for the field. Greatly discouraged, I knew I had to find my *why,* somehow. I was eager to see my passion through to the end. I did not give up. I read more, utilized more resources and consulted with supervisors and professors more; most of all, I reminded myself to believe in *me,* over and above what I saw written on my paper.

You might be wondering what happened. When it was my time to present again; of course, I was very nervous and uncertain. I was not fully sure what my professor would say. If he did not give me positive feedback, I was not sure how I would respond. But I did not give up. Once again, others presented and when it was my time to present I received commendations on some approaches and techniques I utilized with the case I presented. I felt pretty good. I could hardly wait until I returned home to read my professor's comments. The ink was still red, but his response was different. He noted his approval on certain things I said, questions I raised to elicit the patient's insight, accurate diagnoses, treatment plan, and strategies utilized. At the end of my paper my professor wrote: "you finally got your sea-legs!" This was nearly 20 years ago, but I do not think I will ever forget those words, because of how I felt in that moment. My emotions improved, my depressive state lifted. When I discovered *why* I wanted to be able to smile and laugh again, I did what was necessary and *how* to laugh was discovered as well.

The crucible (conformity and compliance)

Conformity and compliance can cause you to feel depressed. Especially if you have an aversion to the two. There are some people who will fight to the death in order to not conform and/or comply. Denying conformity to certain social or familial norms does not necessarily cause any legal consequence; however, not complying with legal matters or certain societal norms as associated with the law can lead to far-reaching, long-standing, consequences. You might be wondering why I chose to add this topic to my book.

I chose to add this topic because there are times when compliance is necessary, even when it seems unfair, but there is wiggle room with conformity. Not conforming might cause you to be ostracized and this can lead to depression, as no one really wants to be isolated due to not conforming. Many times, I work with patients from adolescent age to adult age. Regardless of the age gap; as related to the crucible of conformity and compliance, the response is the same. None of these patients were happy, they presented depressed because they did not want to conform or comply.

How you express non-conformity matters. If you feel strongly about a stance and your position goes against your family, friends, culture, etc., you must decide how you will effectively express your needs without feeling guilty or ashamed, and without denying what you identify as a *need* for you. Whenever a decision is made from a bad emotional place, you will not end up feeling good about the decision.

You will need to make peace with what you desire and accept that some might not agree. If you are a people-pleaser and seek approval from others to feel good emotionally, this will be a challenge for you. It takes strong cognitive skills and emotional intelligence to ride the waves of judgment and ridicule that might come your way, if you decide not to conform. How do you acquire strong cognitive skills and emotional intelligence, you ask? Sometimes it takes rigorous work to implement new ways of thinking and behaving. There is no cookie-cutter approach. Overtime, you discover your new skills. Thus, patience with yourself can be helpful. Surround yourself with positive people and situations, and utilize self-help and professional resources. In doing so, your outcome can be more favorable. Remember, change *can* take significant time; but you are more than worth the investment. Now is the right time to take control of the driving wheel of your life.

Who's driving?

Another thing that can cause you to feel suppressed, oppressed, and depressed is when someone is driving you, in life, where you do not desire to go and at a speed which you are not comfortable. There are very few people, if any at all, that I would feel comfortable enough to fall asleep while they are driving. More often than not I am awake and clinching my seat. I much rather my own driving, thank you! Invariably, when I am in a car and I am the passenger, the driver is either driving too fast, too slowly, too recklessly, or taking a route to a destination that I would not take.

Applying this analogy to life and depression, it is easy to see how you might feel depressed when someone is in the driver's seat of your life. Now, there are some people who either lack confidence or who would rather someone be responsible for their life; I suspect you are not that person. I suspect that you become just as frustrated as I do when others want to lead my life as if they know better about what I need, and they know the course of direction that my life should take. Having said this, let's get into a solution. If someone has been taking charge and steering you around and you have had enough; if you are now depressed about it, get out! Get out of the car and get into the driver's seat of your own life. It might be scary depending on how long you have allowed others to drive you around. You might not feel prepared or confident. Therefore, just as you would not abruptly jump out of a moving vehicle, you might decide to carefully plan your exit. Regardless, there is a sweet sense of independence that accompanies the person who can handle the steering wheel of his and her own life.

The fear of whether or not you are good enough, or smart enough, or strong enough to handle driving your own life might be present; but I assure you, it can be cataclysmic or catastrophic to hand your life over to someone else to make decisions for you. Even if you do not do everything right or perfect, and trust me, you will not; you will do far better by developing confidence as you grow and develop, than by allowing others to navigate and drive your life. So, what will you do?

What is your thing?

- Doing the same thing hoping for different results? Of course, this equals insanity, if you keep doing the same thing that is not getting you what you are after, and you are expecting different results; this is a sign of a sunken place.

- Doing nothing? Feeling immobilized and unable to make decisions? This is another sign of a sunken place.
- Doing anything? Making random moves that do not lead to anything meaningful, fulfilling, and lasting is what you will do from a sunken place.
- So, do something, do not just do nothing or randomly do anything. And whatever you do, stop doing the same thing that is not working, expecting different results. Refuse to become a statistic to this dark, sunken place that is designed to bury you alive.

Buried Alive?

Being in a sunken place can be synonymous to being buried alive. You are very much alive, but a sunken place can leave you with a feeling of being dead, buried. Buried alive! The most difficult thing about being buried alive is that you are still alive, waiting to actually die from suffocation. You feel everything in life as being closed in. Each day and every experience is comparable to another nail that ceils your coffin more tightly. You are aware and alert, you want to scream and shout for help, but nothing comes out. Every day that you do nothing, you are actually succumbing to negativity that is working against you. You will overcome your sunken place; as you learn to use the force of your courage to keep your heart beating, as you exercise the strength of your mind to think yourself beyond the dirt, darkness, and despair, and as you activate the boldness of your will that will motivate you and keep you breathing although the murkiness of depression is trying to talk you into giving up. Being *buried* suggests death, but the word *alive* signifies that you are still filled with power and potential to rise above a sunken place. Even if you feel tapped out and deficient, there is a way out of "the red," a way of out emotional bankruptcy.

Zero Balance, Overdrawn, and Bankrupt?

If you know anything about banking, then you will feel what I am about to say. Even if you have never been at a zero balance, overdrawn on your bank account or you have never filed for bankruptcy, you might be familiar with the terms and know how to avoid the experience.

Let's relate the terms to what it means to be emotionally at zero, overdrawn and bankrupt. These are the times in your life when you continue to give and pour out of your mental and emotional self. You give and you invest until you are depleted. You then wonder why you have lost your zeal, zest, and zing; you wonder why your vitality for life has fizzled out and dwindled away. You can only get out of yourself what is in *you*. Comparable to the banking experience. You might have a bank account opened with your name on it, and you might also have an active account number. However, if you show up to the bank teller or the ATM to make a withdrawal and there are no available funds, you will receive an insufficient fund notification. Just because the account has not been closed, does not mean you can withdraw funds. If you are at a zero balance, you're getting nothing because there is nothing to get; and for sure, if the account stays open too long with a zero balance the institution will close out that account eventually due to no activity on the account. Furthermore, if you have a negative balance, which means you are overdrawn, you will have to pay overdraft fees.

Don't live your life overdrawn. This is not a good feeling financially and it is certainly not a good feeling emotionally. There are some decisions that will be necessary so that you can get out of the negative; but note this, getting out is doable. Regardless of how long you have been "in the red," so-to-speak; you can know excitement for life again. No, I don't know your story; but I do know depression and emotional pain. You see, all pain hurts; regardless of the source. If I bang my elbow on the car door and you fall and scrape your knee, we both feel pain. Our pain might be from a different source, but it is pain nonetheless. I am a firm believer and proponent that you do not have to throw in the towel and sit on the sideline of life. I know you want to get back into the game, even if you cannot imagine the possibility. You have been hovering and you want to land the plane of your life before you run out of fuel and experience a crash landing. Now is a good time to begin to move your feet.

Move your feet to redefine what you stand for

At various times and during different stages and phases of life, redefining what is allowed and tolerated is necessary. Are you at a place in life that you simply need to redefine what you stand for? A montage, if-you-will, including various parts of your life experiences can be mentally compiled for this revision or redefinition. You look back at who you have been, who you are currently, and the person you aspire to be, and you sketch a plan.

Moving your feet: changing your position and direction of interactions and connections is sometimes needful; albeit very painful at times. Only you get to decide what you need. When you reach that point of critical examination and resolution; you will move your head and feet in a different direction. You will redefine what you stand for and what you stand against. As you are faced with this decision of "moving your feet," it is imperative that you gain more self-awareness along the way, so that you are not aimlessly moving your feet. Also, keep this in mind. Coping mechanisms are always at work in your life, even if they do not seem to be the healthiest sometimes; just take note of how you cope as you are making necessary life changes to decrease your depressive symptoms. Consider the following to determine how you cope:

Coping Mechanisms

Below are some coping mechanisms that you might relate to. Coping mechanism are ways that you manage stress. These are not exhaustive, but these coping mechanisms can be helpful in understanding how stress is responded to. All-in-all, the goal of coping is to maintain balance and a state of equilibrium in the mind and emotions. When coping mechanisms are not healthy, then depression can be the outcome of continued stressors. Additionally, when someone is already battling with depression, the chances of utilizing healthy coping skills can be a challenge.

Acting out

When you do not know how to express yourself while experiencing an intense emotion you might "act out." It is important to be able to use your words to express yourself, but when things do not go your way and when you cannot seem to find the words to express yourself appropriately, you might act out. Ways of acting out might include but are not limited to becoming passive-aggressive. This means to acquiesce to someone or something in a passive manner, but there is an aggressive tone to your behavior. Acting out could also include breaking the law, excessive alcohol or substance use, infidelity, breaking curfew, truancy, poor decision-making and indiscriminate behaviors, delinquency of a minor, and so on.

Altruism

This behavior is demonstrated by putting yourself and your concerns to the side in order to exhibit care and concern for the well-being of others. If you are altruistic, you feel good when you put others first. You might not view altruism as a way of managing stress, but according to Harry Mill, PhD., Natalie Reiss, PhD., and Mark Dombeck, PhD., altruism entails socializing and helping; and together these are ways of managing stress. (Mentalhelp.net, 2008). https://www.mentalhelp.net/articles/socialization-and-altruistic-acts-as-stress-relief/. Altruism can be a dysfunction if you are altruistic without life balance. You can be drained very easily if you overextend yourself without balance and boundaries.

Anticipation

With anticipation, you imagine the worst possible thing that could happen, and then anticipate it in order to minimize experiencing the shock factor. There are also times when the anticipation of good events can happen as well. Both are done to manage stress.

Denial

This particular coping mechanism indicates there is a refusal to acknowledge something has happened. This mechanism happens, for sure, in stages of grief and loss. Denial is a common and expected response to traumatic events; whether it is loss through death or the loss of a marital or significant relationship. Also, any other loss that impacts severely enough can lead to denial. Psychotic denial is when there are delusional thoughts associated with the denial.

Devaluation

In order to deal with stress, sometimes underestimating or undermining self and/or others is demonstrated, and to a very magnified degree at times.

Displacement

Displacement is commonly seen with anger. There are times when you might be angry with someone but take it out on someone else who might be a little less threatening than the person you are truly angry toward. For example, you might have had a disagreement with your boss and it angered you; but you go home and yell at the children, the dog, your docile spouse, and the goldfish.

Dissociation

When there is a healthy connection between your awareness, memory, and your perception of yourself and your surroundings, dissociation is not present; however, when you are stressed you might dissociate and lose that connectivity.

Help-rejecting and complaining

I have witnessed this mechanism a few times in my practice. Patients will ask for help, but reject it. They will present with a list of things that are not going right and ask for input. When I explore options with them, the solutions that are apparently viable are dismissed. This is also seen in relationships in families and in the workplace. One person experiencing a hostile interaction with another might ask for help, and then reject the idea.

Humor

I recall a childhood friend who told me one of the most horrific incidents I had ever heard, related to a family matter, and this friend laughed the entire time. I could not help but ask: how do you find that funny? I did not know then what I know now. Humor was used to cope with and manage the stressor, there was also some dissociation going on as well.

Idealization

This is the antithesis to devaluation. With Idealization there are positive qualities used to overestimate a person or self. An example is when you might be dealing with a toxic relationship and the person is abusive to you, but somehow you manage to present that person as treating you better than you are actually treated.

Intellectualization

The individual deals with emotional conflict or internal or external stressors by the excessive use of abstract thinking or the making of generalizations to control or minimize disturbing feelings.

Omnipotence

I call this the God-complex mechanism. The person who deals with the uncomfortable feeling of stress in a way that there is exaggeration about his/her qualities. More often than not the person is masking insecurity, unless the personal is truly delusional and grandiose; which is witnessed with individuals who are diagnosed as bipolar and other psychotic disorders.

Passive-aggressive

Well, I have seen this mechanism throughout my time as a practitioner. When passive-aggressive you might agree to something passively, but in an aggressive behavior. An example might be if you are at odds with someone and that person asks you for something. You might do so, but in an aggressive manner. For example, you are asked: will you bring me something to eat, and then you do so while loudly slamming the pots and dishes, and sloppily preparing the meal.

Projection

Projection is noticed if a person says to you: "I know you think that I don't know what I'm talking about." If you did not actually utter these words to someone, the person might be projecting onto you how he/she thinks, and the person might be attributing negative thoughts to you that he/she thinks toward *self.*

Self-assertion

The individual deals with emotional conflict or stressors by expressing his or her feelings and thoughts directly in a way that is not coercive or manipulative.

Self-observation

The individual deals with emotional conflict or stressors by reflecting on his or her own thoughts, feelings, motivation, and behavior, and responding appropriately.

Splitting

Splitting happens during stressful times, and a person cannot hold two opposing views, so they split. For example, there are good and bad qualities in everyone. When stressed by someone who demonstrates good and bad qualities, the person who splits will identify the person as all good or all bad. I remember dating someone many years ago who told me all good things about his father at one point, he stated that he had no problems with his parents while growing up. Well, later he told me a host of other things about his father such as domestic violence, infidelity, and physical, verbal, and emotional abuse.

He demonstrated difficulty with being able to identify both good and bad qualities in his dad. When I tried to help him to see that his father was comprised of good and bad qualities, I saw how this emotionally and psychologically disturbed him. His mind and emotions could not deal with the stress of it all. He then began to use humor to bring balance and deal with difficult emotions.

Sublimation

This mechanism can be healthy just as long as it is not used to avoid dealing with real issues. Sublimation is about using the energy of stressful events and engaging in some form of exercise, activities, games, etc.

Suppression

As humans we have amazing ways of protecting ourselves from emotional conflict. One way is to suppress. There might be times that you will choose not to think about or deal with any thought, desires, or experiences that add to your stress and emotional upset.

Undoing

You might experience thoughts and emotions, and demonstrate actions that create emotional distress for you, so you fix the problem in your psyche by saying or doing things to counter what you have said or done that caused you emotional discomfort. For example, let's say you had a critical or harshly judgmental thought about a friend who has been nothing but kind to you. The person does not know this, but you feel so badly that you spontaneously do something extra nice to overcome emotional and psychological distress.

These coping mechanisms are ways that you can identify your response to stress. Keep in mind, you might exhibit one or more responses.

According to the National Institute of Mental Health (NIMH), an estimated 16 million adults in the United States had at least one major depressive episode in 2012.

CHAPTER 3

MODERN TIMES AND DEPRESSION

When I consider modern times and depression, my thoughts are sadness. My sadness is because I get to see so much as related to this topic of depression. In fact, I see so much more than the average person. By this I mean that the average person walking around is most likely not walking observing from the angle which I interface and observe; of course, my profession is to do so. And to also interface, observe, engage, and remain updated on changes related to modern times and depression. I am not surprised at all regarding the correlation between depression and our modern times. As time advances, modernity impacts the way people think, emote, and relate to *self* and others in the world. The ultimate goal is to be able to accurately assess and treat patients.

So, is there a correlation between modern times and depression? Research has been conducted on this topic and research continues to support this claim. Overtime; in my 17 plus years of practice I certainly have witnessed changing trends in society, relationship struggles, social media issues, competitiveness in various arenas, and motivation and behavior as related to life in general. One might argue, these factors have always been present in humanity and society. Certainly so; however, there is something about our advancement as a human race that lends itself to more emotional and mental issues.

I have compiled what I have observed during my time as a practitioner, and I repeat, I am not at all surprised at the correlation between modern times and depression. The thing that does baffle me; however, is this: today we are living in much more convenient times, and we have accessibility to all types of resources and opportunities for life advancements. We experience modernity of drive thru and online orders for nearly almost anything you can imagine; such as food, pharmacy, dry cleaning, banking, and I was especially blown away when I found out groceries can be ordered through Amazon. With so many apps available, you can order meals from almost any place. One would think that we would be much more satisfied than we are today, much more emotionally comfortable and stable in our modern times. However, depression is on the rise.

A sense of disconnection that is experienced along with our modern conveniences might explain why depression is on the rise. Also, being connected in an unhealthy manner matters. Take, for example, a string of Christmas lights. This past Christmas I noticed that the string of lights that I hang over my fireplace went out. I could not figure out what was wrong. In searching, I noticed that a few bulbs were burned out and no longer working. Just a few burned out bulbs connected to a string of otherwise functioning bulbs adversely impacted the entire string of bulbs. Connection matters. Whether there is disconnection and isolation, or being connected to someone who is not optimally functioning; these dynamics can create problems for you and impact your emotions, mood, and functioning; and ultimately render you depressed.

Of course, it is important to note that a large number of research points to the conclusion that, more and more, humans are spoiled and desire more and more of a good thing because of an abundance of liberties and opportunities. Thus, when some people do not readily experience good things they become depressed. Additionally, there seems to be less focus on human connectivity and more attention on materialism, thrills, and accomplishments. Even so much more in abundance than our forefathers and foremothers, we currently experience a surplus of material possession and opportunities to accumulate knowledge and wealth. Therefore; for some, there is a sense of entitlement.

This entitlement mentality is noticed mostly in my work with children and teens especially. However, some adults present very entitled and seem to think things ought to go the way they desire simply because they deem it so. I consider such behavior a sense of entitlement not because these individuals desire things to go their way, but because of the anger and control that ensues when things do not go as desired.

Moreover, what is grossly missing in our modern society today is the understanding that there are certain benefits associated with struggle. Just as the experience of the caterpillar that morphs into a beautiful butterfly, a certain amount of struggle is necessary for growth and development, strength, and the ability to soar in life and to soar amid life difficulties. I am not suggesting that you should go around seeking opportunities to struggle; but I am saying: when struggle comes utilize it as a springboard for greater insight, resources, strength, and overcoming ability.

In his writing, *Depression as a Disease of Modernity*, Brandon Hidaka, addressed concerns that our modern times are contributing to depression. Hidaka also points to this concern when he poses this poignant question. "In spite of accumulating material wealth and rising standard of living, why would young people have a higher risk of depression than their parents and grandparents?" Additionally; Hidaka, in his accumulated research, postulates that today's generation is moving more toward social media relationships without traditional social contact, less community involvement, and the focus tends to be more on 'money, status, and appearance.' (Twenge et al., 2010).

Furthermore, according to Hidaka, those who migrate to the United States are less depressed than non-Americans born in the United States, "there seems to be a competitiveness that accompanies our world today that creates more separateness than togetherness." Finally, Hidaka postulates that diet, disease, sleep hygiene, and social environment are all facets of our modern times and these modern times contribute to depression.

I would like to add a couple of other possible reasons for depression:

Immobility

We live in times of ease and convenience that makes a sedentary lifestyle very possible. Being active is a vital component to feeling well emotionally. In fact, when people are severely depressed, if they can just get themselves moving, it is recommended to exercise or go for walks to keep the feel-good chemicals stimulated in the brain. However, with the convenience of being able to take care of most of our needs from the chair at our work desk, being seated in our car, and from the comfort of our couch; it is no wonder why becoming depressed is more likely and overcoming depression is such a challenge.

Of course, I am not suggesting that there are not individuals who are very active; and perhaps you are. What I am highlighting is the link between being active and an improved emotional state. You might ask: are there some people who are active and depressed? I have no doubt, keep in mind; many variables and factors play a role in depression. Another factor is inequity or inequality.

Inequality

When people experience unfairness and biasness, this experience can impact self-esteem; and of course, low self-esteem is a factor associated with depression. Gentrification is very important to some people for various reasons; however, gentrification is only good when underprivileged or disadvantaged individuals are not adversely impacted, when there is no inequity or inequality. In certain regions where there is a high rate of marginalization and underserved individuals, you will most likely find depression.

This example requires a biopsychosocial understanding. Biopsychosocial is a trifecta including the biological, psychological, and social aspects of life. All 3 components play an important part in how well people fare emotionally. Therefore, if there are biological, psychological, and social issues; and add to these socioeconomics issues, the likelihood of depression is very possible. Not a guarantee, but very possible. Let's take a closer look at the biopsychosocial perspective.

The Biopsychosocial Perspective

As you notice the connectivity, you have an opportunity to witness how these areas of life interplay and impact the whole of individuals. It is like a link in a chain. The whole chain is considered no good if a link is broken. In order to get use out of the chain again, you either get rid of the broken link, or repair it.

Social Media

An interesting study was conducted in 2013 by De Choudhury, Gamon, Counts, and Horvitz: Predicting

Depression via Social Media. These researchers found that depressed individuals openly used depressive terms and the number for depressed individuals was higher than non-depressed persons who spoke about depression in general. Also, results revealed that depressed individuals were on social media late nights after 8pm, but not so much for non-depressed people. Researchers suggest this data is in keeping with other, earlier research done in 2000, which suggests depressed people tend to feel symptoms more at nighttime. It was also noted that depressed individuals were not followed and did not follow others as much as non-depressed individuals, suggesting these individuals were more comfortable with a close-knit group of people they could trust and share common experiences.

When I consider my knowledge and experience with social media, I bring a slightly different tone than the other researchers. As I combine both thoughts of how the confidence rate of being able to trust sharing important issues has dropped, as well as the thought that depressed people are able to be located via social media, I also add the idea that there are certain aspects of social media activity that might contribute to depression. Why do I say this? Well, let me first begin by saying that social media is a tool. Social media in and of itself does no harm. However, it is what people do through social media that tends to give rise to many problems.

Here are some issues people experience on social media: infidelity, stalking, harassing, catfishing, social media wars, bantering behaviors, and many more. Also, issues of status, mentions, and number of followers and friends can create a sense of feeling less than. Pics, events, and announcements of weddings, and pregnancies, and promotions, are posted on social media. This can leave others, who cannot relate, feeling left out. But don't worry, just like you are not happy all the time, no one on social media is happy all the time. Do not allow these moments and posts to define what life is really all about. I am not suggesting that people should not feel free to be excited to share. You will do well to take responsibility for what you need to feel emotionally healthy. If this means disconnecting from social media for a period of time, then do what is best for you.

This insertion is mainly to bring awareness that some individuals feel depressed, or more depressed after spending some time on social media. Finally, some people find out unwanted news on social media: such as infidelity, or they learn of a death of a loved one, first on social media (imagine the shock), some people are harassed on social media, and some people are maligned and attacked for their views and/or lifestyles. Again, these all can lead to depression.

Social media of our modern times is not the end all to experiencing a social life and a sense of community. Do not allow yourself to become caught in this web of which there seems to be no escape for some. There are some people who are very good at disconnecting and being able to discipline themselves so that they are not trapped in the social media abyss. If you are not this person, if you find it difficult to break free, and if social media creates emotional discomfort for you; you might consider working social media out of your life for a while. Perhaps when you are stronger and able to utilize social media in a healthy way, you can reengage. Above anything else, do what is good and needful for you. Discover exactly what you need and what is best for you and give it to yourself. One way of getting started on living a balanced life and not succumbing to "depression as a disease of modernity is to think in terms of a sprint versus a marathon.

When runners sprint, they are running at a full speed pace over a shorter distance. However, marathoners run a longer distance over a longer period of time. Think about it. What are you trying to accomplish? Are you trying to keep up with the status quo? How important is it for you to be uniquely who you are and accomplish that which is within your realm of ability? Are you focused on conforming and competing? Only you get to decide, but whatever you do, I suggest considering the benefit of staying in your lane. This does not mean that you should settle for less than your heart desires. No, but just be sure that whatever you are considering; you are not driven by the fast-pace hurriedness of our modern times that keeps individuals on the hamster wheel of life.

I was going through my phone and I found some video voice recordings from nearly four years ago. You see, whenever I take short road trips; I like to take in the scenery and experiences I encounter along the way. I then take a moment to record my experiences. As I scrolled through my phone I came across a recording. During this recording my observation focused on wide versus narrow roads.

I'll begin by stating, night driving is not a good time for me to drive; my night vision is not all that great. While driving one night, I noticed that it was more beneficial for me to focus on the reflectors that divide the lanes on the freeway. As the light from my car illuminated the reflectors I could see what was directly in front of me. I discovered that my night driving experience was much better when I did not try to look too far ahead into the dark, into areas that I could not see clearly. Of course, I noticed others passing me by speedily, they did not seem to have any night-driving issues. But if I focused on others I could have crashed. Little by little as I allowed the light to guide me I got through the darkness and I did not have to strain my eyes, I ultimately reached my destination safely.

So, what does this have to do with depression and our modern times you ask? If you force yourself in a lane that you are not able to manage and you no longer feel good about *you*, you might end up feeling depressed. Make it a point to not look over into the lane of someone else's life. There is so much that you do not know about another's life, and so much that you cannot know; so why bother. And even if you could know about another's life, what good would it do you? You would only end of losing focus of what is going on in your lane, and possibly end up in an accident, so-to-speak. Utilize the light of your internal and external resources to guide your life. As you learn and understand that you are designed to be the best you that you can be, and when you learn to respect, value, and accept that you are awesome and amazing within the realm of your ingenuity, you just might be able to change the somber tide of your life and avoid the trap of this modernity disease called depression.

Depression stems from whole life experiences,
and its effects are far-reaching.

CHAPTER 4

ORIGIN OF DEPRESSION AND DEPRESSION TYPES

Origin of Depression

As you have read thus far, many, many reasons can account for depression. In this chapter you will discover some of the issues that might lead to feelings of depression in a fleeting moment, or a prolonged mood of depression. Some examples of the origin of depression that will be discussed in this chapter are: *situational, medically induced, substance induced, trauma induced, and others.*

Situational

Situational depression results when you deal with situations that are depressing, when you face negative situations and you are not able to think about your situation in such a way that produces a self-soothing effect. Situational depression is as simple as that, by definition; but not always so simple by experience. Of course, experiencing situational depression can be very brief and can subside as soon as a depressing situation changes, but not always. I will share with you a text conversation I had with my sister who relocated from Houston, Texas to the Chicago, Illinois area around the time of the cold holiday season. My sister never claimed to be depressed, so in this example, I am describing what could potentially be a depressing situational experience.

During our conversation, the day after Christmas, 2017; my sister sent me a text message. In her message she exclaimed:

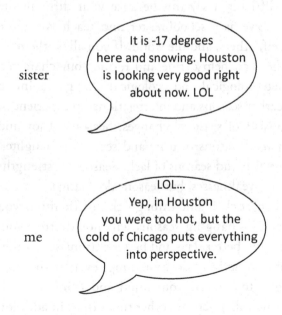

After our back-and-forth text exchange, I came to realize a very poignant point to it all. You see, there are some very wonderful and exciting aspects to cold, snowy weather; especially during the Christmas season. This claim I make is echoed in the sentiment of songs such as "I am dreaming of a white Christmas and Snow is Falling." However, there are times when too much of a good thing can prove to be too much.

From this text discourse I hope you realize that real life is much like the changing weather seasons. There are times when you might appreciate certain aspects of your current life seasons; but at the same time, you might begin to long for other past aspects that you might have taken for granted. Here's the deal: all aspects of your life can be valued even if they are difficult. I say this because your difficult life aspects can serve as a schoolmaster and teach you more about yourself, others, and the world. If you allow them to, difficult times can help define and refine your character. Just like meteorological and ecological changes point to different weather seasons and interrelationship experiences, your life consists of seasonal changes. Seasons of joy and seasons of pain. Seasons of tears and seasons of laughter. Seasons of wealth and seasons of lack. Seasons of strengths and seasons of weaknesses; but seasons do change.

If you can stick it out through the difficulties, you will realize that changing seasons will not destroy you. Yes, experiencing better days and better seasons sometimes require that you actively do something, even if the only active thing is to exercise your mind and think yourself into a better mood. There are other times that, in addition to changing the way you think, you also have to practically make life changes to experience better seasons.

For example, you might have to make changes regarding a job, or education, or budgeting, or parenting, or nutrition and health, or marital relationship interactions, dealing with stressful relationships in general, and so many more situations might describe necessary changes in order to experience more enjoyable life seasons. If you can stick it out through life changes, you might avoid becoming utterly overwhelmed, depressed, and sunken. Because in reality, regardless of the seasons of life or seasons of the universe, the changing of seasons can add to your life lessons and your growth and develop if you allow them.

Experiencing situational depression can be just as debilitating as experiencing depression due to a chemical imbalance in the brain or any other more severe type of depression. Situational depression can range from mild to severe depending on what the situation is. For example, if a situation is such as a job change that you did not adjust to quite so well. Perhaps you thought the experience would be different and it is actually depressing. If your thought processes and your ability to address adjustment issues can happen sooner rather than later, you might be less likely to experience severe depression. Perhaps you will remain at a mild range of depression, because the situation does not linger.

Now, let's say your situation is a change in a significant relationship that is very dear to you, or a huge financial change that significantly alters your life. These are situations of a different kind. If you do not possess the necessary self-soothing tools or coping strategies to adjust to such stressful situations, you might end up at the moderate to severe range of depression. Again, preparedness, along with proper mental adjustments can help you avert sinking into deep depression.

Just as when you are dealing with events of grief and loss due to the death of a loved one, you can also experience the same stages of grief and loss as related to situational changes. According to Elizabeth Kubler Ross, the stages of grief loss and loss include the following D.A.B.D.A:

Denial
A state of disbelief that what has happened truly happened. A shocking and numbing state.

Anger
Furious, vexed, and holding the idea that whatever is happening should not be happening.

Bargaining
Turning over and over in the mind how things could have turned out differently. Feeling some regret and resentment. Possibly playing the mind game of if I could have, I would have, I should have.

Depression
Overwhelming sadness that leaves you heavy, exasperated and gasping for breath at times.

Acceptance
A place in the stages of grief and loss where you finally realize things are what they are. The anger can subside, the bargaining can end, and you, for sure, are no longer in denial.

Other ways grief and loss are experienced include but are not limited to: an ideal that might not have the possibility of being realized, or any other significant phase of life concern such as aging, aging parents, infertility, becoming empty nesters, and so on. When situational depression is experienced, the stages of grief and loss are applicable to getting to the place of acceptance and resuming a fulfilling life again.

Medically induced

Medically induced depression simply means a depressive state that is brought on by medical issues. Depression as a result of a medical issue can include any side effects of certain medical issues, as well as medication prescribed to treat medical issues. For example, medical conditions such as kidney disease, lupus, arthritis, HIV/AIDS, multiple sclerosis, hypothyroidism, heart disease, and many others. As well as medications to treat medical issues, such as: beta-blockers that are prescribed for hypertension or high blood pressure, corticosteroids that are prescribed for inflammation and treats such medical issues as arthritis, lupus, and gout. Such medications lower serotonin levels and can contribute to depression. Benzos are another class of medications that can cause depression. Benzos depress the central nervous system.

Some hormone replacement therapy drugs can alter the mood and cause depression. Researchers also suggest that prolonged use of dopamine can cause depression; therefore, such medications to treat ADHD, such as Ritalin and Provigil should be considered. Some other drugs are anti-seizure medications, medications that are prescribed for hyperlipidemia or elevated cholesterol, and some medications to treat gastrointestinal issues and irritable bowel syndrome.

Substance induced

Substance induced depression can be brought on through the use of drugs such as cocaine, meth (or any other stimulants), marijuana, LSD, steroids, solvents, and ketamine. Also, drugs such as heroin and other opioids, and alcohol. Any such substances impact the brain by causing chemical changes and can result in severe depression. In the case of withdrawing from opioids, depression is a very common side effect. There are times when individuals might use depressants and alcohol to quell anxiety, but these very same drugs can cause depression. For example, ecstasy (MDMA) can help with the feeling of anxiety, but the after effect is a feeling of depression due to the depletion of serotonin in the brain.

Trauma induced

Extreme stress symptoms that are not resolved following a trauma can lead to depression. The reason is that reliving trauma in the mind and not being able to escape the memories and even nightmares that are associated with trauma, can cause feelings of overwhelming sadness and hopelessness that anything about the trauma will change. Of course, the trauma itself will never change or be undone. However, the hard work of overcoming the memories and effects of the trauma takes place in the mind. When the mind is stuck the more likely depression is to linger. There is a desperation to feel better emotionally, but relief cannot be experienced until the mind is healed.

Others

Other factors that contribute to depression are hormonal changes in men and women, postpartum; and other medical issues such as chronic pain, cancer or other major, chronic medical issues. These factors are placed in a separate category because it is appropriate to discuss how severe and chronic medical issues impact the self-image and self-esteem of individuals. As a result, individuals might experience depression. In the previous section of medically induced depression, I discussed medications that are prescribed which can make depression an even more, compounding issue.

Which leads to the concern of depression and suicide for those individuals who live with chronic medical conditions for which there is no cure. When individuals see no hope for a quality of lifestyle they would desire, and when individuals experience relationship issues and loneliness as a result; they are more likely to experience suicidal ideation as a way out of the physical and emotional pain.

There are many examples of the origin of depression that are without individuals' control and of course, there are some choices and behaviors that individuals can control to avoid depression. The following reading will provide insights to help you gain perspective on ways you might not have considered when you think about the origin of depression.

Diet

Inadequate protein intake

Research from the National Institutes of Health suggests that adequate amounts of protein intake plays a significant role in the way the brain functions and in experiencing mental health.

Too much trans-fat

An article is published in Psychology Today, Trans-fats: Bad for your brain, 2015. In this article, Diane Roberts Stoler, Ed.D reports that trans-fat can lead to serious health complications including heart disease, cancer, diabetes, low birth rate, obesity, and immune dysfunction. Stoler reports that food such as processed foods, fried foods, salad dressings, muffins, chips, cookies, and baked goods that are processed and store-bought include trans-fat; and trans-fat destroys cells, weakens hormones, and reduces serotonin; ultimately impacting brain functioning, and thereby adversely affecting the mood. As a result, depression can be experienced.

If you can recall back in our previous reading, the issue of serotonin depletion as related to drugs and medication was also mentioned. Additionally, a study conducted at University Department of Epidemiology and Public Health monitored adults for a span of 5 years and discovered a link between sweets, fried foods, processed meats, starchy snacks, boxed cereal and a higher rate of depression.

Not enough health fats

The truth about fats is a published article from Harvard Health Publishing: Harvard Medical School. Updated in

August 2017. Good fat or healthy fats are identified as fats that are rich in Omega 3 and 6, nuts, and beans. Of course, as indicated above, it is important to not eat these foods in processed form. It is well noted that foods that are most unhealthy tend to be the foods that are least expensive. These insights are for your learning and understanding, to become more aware of the high correlation between diet and depression.

Carbohydrates

Simple carbohydrates are what you want to limit in your diet. These are items such as: candy, cookies, processed baked items, sodas, energy drinks, drinks with high fructose corn syrup, and certain ice cream items just to name a few. These carbohydrates impact your blood sugar levels. *Complex* carbohydrates include, vegetables such as broccoli, leafy greens and carrots, grains, fruit that are rich in fiber especially. Complex carbohydrates are a good source of fiber and other important nutrients, unlike some simple carbohydrates.

In addition to your diet intake, be sure to visit your physician regularly as scheduled and keep your blood levels checked. I mention this because there are times, for one reason or another, that blood work might reveal deficiencies that could impact health. When deficiencies are experienced, sometimes individuals supplement with the wrong foods, drinks, and vitamins, and matters are worsened. Also, it is important to note here: I am fully aware that some reading this material might be under treatment or medical advice from a professional.

This material is not intended to treat or change any

treatment regimen or plan you are following. Be sure your medical provider is made aware of any changes that could impact your treatment. Also, always be sure to stay up and current on your doctor visits as scheduled and as needed. If you feel a little off with your energy, sleep, mood, etc., and something does not feel quite right, schedule a visit.

Sedentary lifestyle

Get moving! Research reveals that movement is very important to feel good chemicals in the brain and can have a positive impact on your mood. In the world today, most of what we do as human being does not require a lot of movement and exertion of physical activity. You name it: you can avoid walking around and standing in lines at the grocery store because you can purchase groceries online for delivery. There are drive up windows for pharmacy, dry cleaning, food, banking or online banking. There is online dating and online sex or sexting, so people do not go out as much and meet others in the way people once established and cultivated relationships. Education (on all levels) can be accomplished online.

Life and lifestyles are setup today so that people hardly have to leave home anymore. Of course, there are work-from-home options, right? Also, there are doctor home visits for minor medical issues and you can get your prescription without leaving the home. It is no wonder so many people are depressed. Life is such today that we can be a recluse without a second thought. In fact, we can become a recluse without intention. Sometimes it just ends up being an easier choice and before you know it individuals are deciding to engage less and less in the conventional way of living and being in the world and in society.

According to the aforementioned article, 'The disease of modernity,' it is suggested that the modern culture in which we live creates this sense of aloneness and seclusion. The article further suggests that individuals in cultures such as Amish are less depressed because they rely on one another for emotional support.

Life dissatisfaction

There are many reasons to be dissatisfied in life, you don't really have to look hard to find a reason. Dissatisfaction can result from unrealized dreams, unresolved past trauma or life events, relationship stress and strain, medical issues, parenting concerns, stressful employment, and financial difficulties, general phase of life concerns, stages of development challenges, and life transitions; you name it, and just about anything can create life dissatisfaction. However, perception and perspective can make a difference.

Some time ago I read a book: Think Yourself Happy. I agree that this is a possibility, for those with appropriate cognitive ability. However, I also know that how some individuals arrive at "happy," might require additional tools other than thinking, be it temporarily or for the long haul. There definitely are no hard and fast rules as related to the mind and emotions; but for sure, the mind and emotions must work in tandem to accomplish the goal of a good and healthy mood state.

*The Diagnostic Statistical Manual (DSM)
for Mental Illness Identifies the many forms
of depressions and their subtypes, lending
insight to how intricate depression can
be, as well as providing understanding
for those who suffer from depression.*

Depression Types

Bipolar, seasonal affective disorder, agitated depression, dysthymia (persistent depressive disorder), major depressive disorder, depressive disorder, NOS, Post-Partum Depression, and Premenstrual dysphoric disorder.

Bipolar Depression

Bipolar depression is a part of bipolar disorder. When experiencing episodic lows or the depressive side of bipolar disorder, one might experience sadness, fatigue, loss of pleasure regarding experiences that were once enjoyed, changes in appetite and weight, difficulty focusing, concentrating, and making decisions.

Seasonal Affective Disorder or SAD

This disorder is characterized by depressive symptoms that are experienced during the same time each year. This diagnosis is related to season changes. Symptoms are usually experienced consistently during the same season during the year. Please note, with all diagnoses; there must be a significant impairment in functioning.

Agitated depression

This particular type of depression is formerly known as melancholia agitata. Individuals experiencing agitated depression might appear restless and angry. Agitated depression is not typically a manifestation of lethargy and feelings of sadness. Individuals might feel keyed up and experience difficulty winding down. Some individuals with agitated depression might engage in risk taking behaviors, and are more likely to engage in road-rage and more frequent interpersonal conflicts at home, work, or school.

Dysthymia (persistent depressive disorder)

Dysthymia is a mild form of chronic depression. With dysthymia there are fewer met symptom criteria as related to a major depressive disorder, and the symptoms are not as severe as with a major depressive disorder. Symptoms are present for 2 years for adults and 1 year for children. With this diagnosis, mania, hypomania, or cyclothymia are not present, along with any other diagnoses such as schizophrenia and schizoaffective disorder.

Major Depressive Disorder

With major depression there is the experience of a persistent depressed mood, lasting at least 2 consecutive weeks, including at least 5 out of 9 symptoms, such as, but not limited to a loss of interests in once enjoyed activities, sadness, feeling worthless, thoughts of death, and so forth. Symptoms impact and impair daily life, and are not better accounted for by other psychotic disorders.

Depressive Disorder NOS or Unspecified

An unspecified or not otherwise specified (NOS) depressive diagnosis simply suggests that an individual is experiencing depressive symptoms but does not meet the full criteria for other depressive disorders.

Post-Partum Depression (PPD)

In the most recent DSM 5 version, anyone qualifying as experiencing post-partum depression must first be diagnosed as having a major depression disorder, and then meet the symptoms requirement for peripartum-onset specifier (*thoughts of hurting yourself or your infant, insomnia, bouts of tearfulness, anxiety, fear, guilt, and inability to carry out activities of daily living*). If you have a history of depression or schizoaffective disorder, you are at a higher risk of experiencing post-partum depression. PPD can be diagnosed when symptoms, after giving birth, persist consecutively for 2 weeks.

Premenstrual Dysphoric Disorder (PMDD)

This diagnosis is added for your understanding of what is considered beyond symptoms of a normal menstrual cycle. Of course, all women are different and experience symptoms differently, but PMDD is a diagnosis for what one might experience that goes beyond normal experiences of a menstrual cycle. Included in the symptoms criteria are depressive symptoms. While some of these symptoms are typical for what is normally expected during a menstrual cycle (anxiety, depression, restlessness, moodiness, tearfulness, outburst, and anger just to name a few), PMDD is diagnosed when symptoms are severe enough to impair functioning and relationships.

*There is treatment and hope for
those who experience depression,
you don't have to do it alone.*

CHAPTER 5

TREATMENT MODALITIES AND APPROACHES

Treatment Modalities

Individual therapy

Individual therapy involves one person. The individual generally presents to work on issues that might include relationships with others, but chooses to do so alone.

Group therapy

Group therapy involves multiple persons working through similar concerns such as depression, grief and loss, phase of life changes, workplace and relationship stress, etc.

Medication services

This particular modality is usually an adjunct to other therapy modalities. When it seems appropriate, my patients are referred for a medication evaluation to determine medication necessity.

Conjoint family therapy

Family therapy proves helpful when working with families related to parenting issues, parent and children issues, sibling issues, and when helping families with children who experience depressive symptoms and any other issues that impair functioning at home and/or school. Family therapy is also utilized in working with all adult family members who are stuck in dysfunction, unresolved issues, and depression.

Couple's therapy

When addressing depression within the context of a couple's relationship, there are times when one partner is depressed and the symptoms impact the relationship. Then there are times when relationship dynamics are stressful, and relationship dynamics create depression.

Treatment approaches

In these approaches is the possibility for an eclectic approach.

Cognitive Behavioral Therapy (CBT)

CBT is a psychotherapy treatment that focuses on the correlation between thoughts, emotions, and behavior. Using this approach, you can learn how your thoughts impact your emotions, and ultimately the way you behave and interact with *self* and others. Reframing is a strategy I use often, in helping patients improve their mood, by changing their perspective.

Dialectical Behavior Therapy (DBT)

DBT, coined by Dr. Marsha Lenehan, is a form of cognitive behavioral therapy that was originally used to treat those who were chronically suicidal. DBT focuses more on balancing acceptance and change. Acceptance involves mindfulness and distress tolerance, and change involves emotion regulation and interpersonal effectiveness. In its most simple definition, dialectical means to integrate or bring opposites together. In order to deal with distress effectively, you must be able to integrate opposing thoughts in your psyche.

Solution Focused

Solution-focused therapy is just that—being focused on solutions that helps you to reach your goals and minimize emotional and mental discomfort. With this approach, I generally work with patients to think about solutions by focusing on strengths and what is already working and going well.

Interpersonal therapy (IPT)

This therapeutic approach is short-term, approximately 3-4 weeks. The focus is on treating mood disorders. IPT is designed to address distressful issues and improve interpersonal and social functioning.

Psychodynamic therapy

This approach is insight-oriented. The focus is on the impact that past and current events have on functioning, exploring what changes are desired, and identifying what steps are necessary in order to attain desired therapeutic goals.

Play therapy

I utilize play therapy when working with depressed children, adolescents, and some teens. Play is the language of children. While I desire that everyone, even adults, would appreciate the power of play, some adults and teens come into the office so very serious and overcome with depression, playing does not appeal them. There is a therapeutic attempt to play therapy. Once people are able to relax, enjoy play, and feel the carefreeness side of life; being able to explore and open up is more likely to be experienced.

Effective ways to overcome negativistic and depressive thinking

Change the negative thoughts in your head

In a very frustrated manner, individuals will ask: "so how do I do that?" My answer is: It takes time and practice to reconstruct negative patterns. Such as if one is building a house. You must first have in mind the design and pattern of what you are building, then you must possess tools. Patterns and tools are half the battle. Next, you must begin to apply what you know. Nothing that is worth building and nothing that is built solidly and securely will be done overnight.

I am sometimes upset when I see construction going on

for years when a new bridge is being built because it creates a lot of traffic. But to be honest, if a bridge is built too quickly, it would take the strength of a mighty army to force me to drive across it. I want to know that time and quality effort has been put into being sure the job is done effectively.

Entertain me a little, try to think in these terms. The value you affix to your life is what will guide your thinking and emotions. So, have you thought about this, or do you already know that the rental price for a high-end car is about the full purchase price of an average car? In some places, a Bugatti rents for $25,000 per day. Also, when you scan restaurants, drive-thru fast food restaurants and 5-star restaurants are all categorized as restaurants, but these restaurants are separated by their kind, class, and value. If you are hungry, you might eat at a high-end restaurant, or a fast food drive-thru and you will satisfy your hunger.

However, your experience will not be the same. You see, fast food restaurants can compete amongst themselves, but they cannot compete with more high-quality dining and cuisine. Let me be clear, this is not about what you can afford to eat or drive, or what you are willing to spend on cars and food. My point is to illustrate value and *you*.

Ask yourself: are you a Bugatti or a buggy? A Porsche or a Pontiac? A Rolls Royce or a Range Rover? A Lamborghini or a Lacrosse? A Maserati or a Mitsubishi? A Jaguar or a Jackal? All of these vehicles will get you from point A to point B, but quality can make a difference.

Eye-level Picking

I recall a time when I was in school for my undergraduate, business degree, one of my professors taught us how items are set up at the grocery store to draw attention to people when they are shopping. This was many years ago, but I never forgot. As I began compiling data for this manuscript, the term, eye-level picking, came to mind. I will explain what I mean by eye-level picking, but first I will go back to the example of what I learned while pursuing my degree.

My professor indicated that we (his students) should take notice the next time we are in a grocery store. He said we should go to the cereal aisle and notice how the boxes are placed on the shelves. He was correct. The sweet cereal with cartoons were placed at eye-level for children. I did mention this was years ago, right? Well, that strategy has to be a working strategy because it is still designed this way today. In 2017, an article was published by someone at Cornell University's Food and Brand Lab, Charles H. Dyson School of Applied Economics and Management; and what did I see as I read this article? I saw these words: adult cereals are placed straight ahead, and twice as high as children's cereal. Children's cereal, with characters on the box, look down at a 9.6-degree angle. Findings were that children connected more with cereal when making eye contact with the character on the box.

Of course, we know that most of the sugary cereals are not good for children. Especially with the colors and dyes added. However, these are impressionable children and they will want what they see that appeals to the eye. Now, let's turn our focus back to eye-level picking. You know, that type of picking we tend to do as humans. If he or she looks good enough to the eye, we might go for it. Let's take it a step further. If you are not in a good place emotionally, you might be depressed, might be lonely, experienced a break-up, dating is not all it is made out to be, and you are experiencing a difficult time; and you are indeed lonely and feeling empty and distraught.

Someone comes along from a low place and finds you looking in a low place because you are depressed and your gaze is cast downward, and you choose from this low place. If you are not feeling good about yourself and if you are depressed; you will pick from your eye-level. It is always a good rule of thumb to not allow yourself to embrace anyone closely while you are downcast and vulnerable. Give yourself time to get into a better picking position, when your gaze is upward and you feel good about yourself. Take care of *you* and then you place yourself in a good position to pick upward.

What do you have an appetite for?

I am not referring to food and drink. What do you have a mental and emotional appetite for? What is your daily intake that either fuels you or drains you? What you entertain and who you embrace does matter and can determine if you will feel good about yourself. If there is no biological base only, depression is about how you think about yourself and others, and how you relate to yourself and others. What you have an appetite for will let you know if you are healthy in your thinking and emotions and can be a barometer for your quality of life and overall well-being.

Rid yourself

Reduce the amount of contact with those who do not serve as a positive support system for you. Subsequently, surround yourself with those who encourage and inspire you. Rid yourself of surroundings that create a somber feeling for you. It is also important to understand the value of conversations, music, movies, foods, and beverages, and any other habits and unhealthy coping you might have engaged in that does not help add to a positive euthymic mood; but rather, perpetuates your dysphoric mood. Rise above, move forward, and don't look back, except for times when you glance back quickly to remember how strong you are to have overcome.

For example, let's consider the rearview mirror in your vehicle. Your rearview mirror is for looking at what is behind you without the need to turn your ahead. There are pros and cons to looking back through your rearview, and you should do so with skill and precision. For example, when you must look behind to transition over to another lane; you use your rearview mirror. Some people turn their head to look back, but this can be dangerous. Accidents can happen more swiftly than you will be allowed enough time to turn around and back again. Therefore, the rearview mirror comes in handy, it only requires a quick shifting of your eyes and you can still see peripherally and ahead, while quickly glancing back. Again, as I said, this requires skill.

Looking back in the life of your past is much the same. When you have decided that you will take a look back, take a glance; and not-so-much a long stare. This is in reference to looking back at good and bad memories. Here is why. Looking back too long at bad experiences can cause depression. You might begin to experience regret, resentment, shame, guilt, and the like. If you will look back, take a glance to see what you can do differently; but also, look back to view how far you have advanced in spite of how grim things might look.

In reference to looking back at things that have been good and favorable. You might ask: what could be bad about looking back on favorable memories? What tends to be an issue with looking on favorable memories is the possibility of reminiscing and getting stuck on what was good and enjoyable at a given point and time, and becoming stuck and depressed about how things might have changed.

For example, the loss of a loved one: a parent, a spouse, a child, sibling, etc., might cause you to become stuck if you keep looking back at what was (the good moments that are over) can prevent you from moving forward. This could also be true for empty nesters when children grow up and leave the home, depression could be experienced due looking back too long. This could also be true for stages of human development as we age and look back at our youthful days, looking back too long and remembering when things were easier or better, or more fun and carefree, can create depressive symptoms as well. Being able to rid yourself of anything that sets you back and holds you back is key to overcoming negativistic and depressive thinking.

Relax

Cultivate a healthy mindset of balance that promotes overall and holistic health in your life. Cultivate a mind and heart of gratitude (eliminate bickering, complaining, and making excuses). You get to decide how relaxing is defined. Of course, healthy relaxation strategies would be in keeping with your desire and goal to improve your emotions and lift your depression. Be sure that you are able to locate environments, atmospheres, activities, and relationships that add to your improved mood and not things that detract.

Set goals

Regularly challenge yourself to do something new. This is a good way to strengthen your brain, self-confidence, mood, and so on. Be sure to complete your goals and refrain from setting goals that are unattainable. Be realistic. One way that I train myself to learn something new is to drive to local areas that I have never been. I fill my gas tank and just drive, trying not to rely on my GPS. In doing so, I force my brain to problem-solve and learn new information. Of course, I am careful to pick appropriate times of day and keep safety in mind. This is my way of setting goals to intentionally challenge myself to think outside of my routine way of thinking, and at times I have saved myself from becoming stuck in a routinized lifestyle that could lead to blah feelings.

Imagine your possibilities

Give back. Locate someone or something to invest in. Volunteer. Research has proven that giving into the lives of others tend to have a positive impact on the brain and mood. When others express gratitude to you, the pleasure center of your brain processes this data and you feel pleasure. With this interchange, your mood lifts and you can begin to realize things about yourself that you might have forgotten; for example, you might begin to remember how wonderful and valuable you are. You might also begin to anticipate how much more meaning you can contribute to your own life, to the lives of others, and perhaps impact much wider and larger realms than you imagined before.

*Your depression story is uniquely yours,
but it can significantly help others.*

CHAPTER 6

CASE EXAMPLE

Justin's Story

The Start

Justin was born to Florence Smart in 1961, he was born with German Measles and Red Measles, and suffered brain damage; ultimately cerebral palsy ensued. Justin was introduced to our family through my brother, when I was only a child. It seemed he became like a family member instantly. We all loved him and included him as part of the family. Justin and I have journeyed throughout the years, encouraging each other. Although our lives took different paths; we always managed to reconnect periodically and catch up as if no time was lost at all. I consider it an absolute privilege to have Justin share his story by way of this writing.

During an interview with Justin he stated: "I noticed I was different from everyone around me when I was in the first grade." Hear what Justin spoke to me during his interview: It was first grade at Florence J. Chester Elementary School, I was wearing leg braces and during that time I noticed people staring at me. Staring did not only come from other children, but adults stared as well. When I speak of different, I was the only child in school who had to wear short pants due to wearing my leg braces, it did not matter the time of year or season, I had to wear short pants.

Not only were school days difficult, but after school was difficult because I had hard conversations with my mother about my diagnosis of cerebral palsy and why I was different, I had lots of questions, as you could imagine. I was only 6 years old, I was different, and I did not know why. However, I trusted that my mother knew, and so hard conversations were had. I was so very young and there were so many experiences surrounding my disability, but one thing for sure that does not escape, the incredible feeling of sadness.

I am grateful that my mother was there for me, she was very spiritual, not only was she spiritual; but she was very patient, and a great listener and encourager. My mother spoke to my possibilities and potential and the way she handled me caused me to believe in myself. Other events such as being on the cover of Transit Rider's Digest in 1967, and having The United Way select me as the United Way poster child certainly added to my self-esteem as well.

It is important for me to give you information about the conditions I grew up living in. I grew up in subsidized public housing, and I lived there until I was at least 15 or

16 years of age. If you know anything about public housing, or government housing known as the "projects," you could only imagine that challenge in and of itself. I recall children teasing me and laughing, mocking the way I walked and wanting to fight.

Today, as an adult, I understand it as their ignorance to what was really going on with me, but as a child I could not see the whole picture. As a result, my biggest challenge aside from the physical and emotional struggle, was the challenge of having to physically fight. I now realize that I initiated some of the fights because of anger, and I knew that I was being mistreated. I wanted it to stop and fighting seemed the only way to make it happen, to stand up for myself.

The Struggles

As I approached adolescent and teen years, my struggles mounted. Beginning junior high was pivotal for me. Of course, it would be because it is a very challenging time in the life of a child in general, now imagine a child with a physical disability. Keep in mind, I am still wearing braces on my legs and I am still wearing short pants year-round, even in the coldest, most inclimate weather.

During this time, I was more self-aware and I was more in-tuned with the direction in which I wanted my life to go; well, I was as in-tuned as one could be considering I was only a budding adolescent. The desire to feel more like a normal kid, to be like everyone else around me, was heightened during this stage of development; especially when it came to girls and my desire and love to play football. Also, I wanted to learn to ride a bike like other kids around me. I was always eager to do what seemed impossible for me, so that I could avoid the pain of feeling different. I finally did learn to ride a bike and I learned to ride with braces on my legs. My mother, who has always been my greatest supporter, would allow me to take my braces off at 5pm to be able to play football.

Additionally, I strongly desired to have a girlfriend, but this was scary for me. The greatest challenge was the struggle of approaching a girl and the horrifying thought of being rejected. Although I was different in the sense of having a physical disability; everything else about me as growing boy, a male growing into a man, was developmentally correct. Everything in me wanted to be with girls.

Here is another challenge, I had to go to physical therapy four days after school, on public transportation. The most difficult physical experience during these times included two bus transfers, traveling alone in the dark, and the excruciating pain associated with actually doing the physical therapy exercises. Imagine this, I traveled alone, at times in the cold and dark, within an 8-block radius roundtrip, and this was after all of the physical exertion of bus transfers and exercising at my doctor appointments.

At times I felt very humiliated. Out of frustration, there were times I did not attend my set appointments. I wanted to feel a sense of normalcy, so I would skip my appointments and go to the pool hall. At the pool hall no one seemed to see me as "different." It became my escape; not to mention that I enjoyed these regularly skipped appointments to have some "me-time" at the pool hall, and this led to me ultimately becoming very proficient at playing the game of pool.

The Shift

My shift began in high school. During this time, I had more friends. Talking to girls was not as awkward as before. I cannot pinpoint exactly when it happened for me, but I noticed that my confidence had grown. Having the freedom from my braces was a plus. My 9th grade year was when my doctor assessed that my physical ability had improved to the point that my braces were no longer necessary. Here are some of my experiences that happened during my shift, and continued to add to my self-confidence:

- Driving—driving was a very interesting experience for me. My high school had driver's education. The challenge was whether or not the school board would allow me to take driver's education, because of possible liability concerns. After a lot of arduous paperwork, and my mother and my doctor working diligently to help me get through the process; I was approved to take driver's education. All eyes were on me. *Unbelievable* is the look I saw on everyone's face. I practiced driving my entire senior year and I received my driver's license in 1979. I was so excited and I was able to drive to my senior prom.

- Dating—my very first date was in 1979, I met a girl named Brenda. She accompanied me to my senior dance. This was my very first girlfriend and my very first heartbreak.

- Socialization—my social life was just like any other person my age. I hit the clubs, enjoyed going to movies, continued to play pool, attempted to play basketball, and would also engage in bowling. As high school years ended, I entered life as a man. Because of my fondness for sports, I desired to go on and become a sportscaster as an adult.

The Successions

While my desire after high school was to go on and become a sportscaster, my life took a different direction. Instead, I became a student at Delgado Community in 1981 and studied Business Administration and ultimately receive an Associate Degree in 1983. During my studies at Delgado, I also became gainfully employed with a reputable cable company—Cox Cable. This period of my life was exciting and challenging. I did not have my own vehicle initially; therefore, I had to use public transportation. There were times when walking and standing were a challenge, carrying heavy books, people overlooked me. I had to stand on a moving bus, while experiencing difficulty balancing myself. Eventually I invested in a Moped, and this eased some of the pressure and tension.

During my successive years as a college student and employee, my social life soared. I partied and enjoyed going out with my peers and I felt included. Despite the struggles of my earlier years, as I think on my journey, up to this point in my reflections; I am grateful.

Another milestone in my life that I am very proud of is the moment that I announced my calling to the ministry and received my licensure as a minister. These events happened somewhere around the early 1990s, and from that time on, I enjoyed the opportunity to honor God and serve others in ministry. With all the bountiful blessings God has given me, even with challenge, I count it a privilege to be able to give back and demonstrate gratitude.

Although I dated off-and-on throughout my college years, at some point I met the woman who would eventually become my wife and the mother of my daughter (JuVrelle Smart). My marital relationship lasted for nearly 8 years, I am grateful for having had an opportunity to experience being a husband for such a time; and of course, I experience abundant gratitude because my role as a father is for a lifetime.

The Sentiments

As I have segued to this section of my journey, I would be negligent if I do not take this opportunity to mention my siblings: Janice, James, and Eugene. Janice played a vital role in my childhood. Being the eldest sibling, she was the first sibling with financial ability and emotional support to contribute to my childhood, along with my mother. In general, James was with me in elementary school, he also accompanied me when I attended my doctor appointments.

Additionally, there were times when James physically fought for me when I experienced altercations. Eugene was also supportive and demonstrated care and concern as we were growing up; and even till this very day, my siblings are still supportive. In recognition of my gift, my beautiful daughter; JuVrelle Smart, who is the apple of my eye. I am very blessed to have her in my life. From a very tender age, she understood her dad. She has always looked out for me and defended me in many ways.

At a glance, as you have taken a peek into my life, I have spoken from a point of being supported as well as shared my struggles and challenges. However, I do not want to leave you without expressing those moments of darkness, primarily because this book is about understanding and addressing depression. For me, depression was felt and recognizable during times I lost interested in caring for my surroundings.

I am a person of order and organization; therefore, when I would allow things to get out of order and out of control (such as activities of daily living) I knew I was depressed. Also, I withdraw when I am depressed. I isolate from those closest to me. I am much quieter and disconnected. These bouts of depression happened periodically throughout my past life, and can still happen today if I do not take the time to be proactive and notice what is going on internally and externally.

There were times that family, and nothing and no one else could understand or help me through. There were times in my personal, human development that I had to deal with *me*, without being able to feel comfort, at times not even comfort from God. With this being said, all along I knew that if I was going to get through, it was going to be by faith, spiritually speaking.

This does not mean that I was not responsible to do some things in my humanity. I had to practically put some thoughts and behaviors into action in order to demonstrate my faith, faith that I knew coming out of the dark place was a real possibility. A bible scripture that has helped was: "they that wait upon the Lord shall renew their strength." This scripture has always been a help to me and continues to be of great strength to me today.

I encourage you to always believe in yourself, regardless

of what you face in life. If you think this will help, I allow you to use my statement I use to pick myself up when I am down: "I got to get back up on the horse, I got to keep going." Mountains of life issues might seem insurmountable at times, and in all reality, there are some things that are difficult to hurdle over. I recall times when I felt alone in my situation and emotional and physical pain. I have felt trapped, like no one could possibly understand what I deal with. There are times that I can feel this way today. Nevertheless, I have come to depend on the scripture that encourages me to remember that the things that are not possible for me to do in my human strength are things that are possible for God to do. I also encourage you to rely on external resources that are available through various community agencies, counseling, and various other electronic resources to serve as guides and provide a sense of direction.

Finally, I am honored to know this author and to have been acquainted with her for many years. To have been asked to share my story is gratifying and I hope that my story, even if in only a small way, can be a blessing to you and that you can gain hope and strength as you learn to laugh again; as you go on with understanding and addressing depression.

*What you don't know can hurt
you—increase your awareness of
the implications of depression.*

CHAPTER 7

IMPLICATIONS OF DEPRESSION

Implications of depression are far-reaching. Many aspects of your life are impacted when you are depressed. Depression can be stifling and can leave you feeling as if you are alone, inside of your pain while at the same time, pain resides within you. Some implications that will be discussed in this chapter are: *hopelessness, relationship issues with self, others, and your environment, low motivation or extreme busyness, suicidal thoughts and/or suicide, poor coping, and hospitalizations.*

Hopelessness

Hopelessness can be an abiding debilitating experience that looms like a dark cloud. It casts doubt that any possibility of better days is possible. Hopelessness eats away at the mind and emotions like cancer. Eventually, if it lingers, hopelessness can impact your physical health. It robs you of creativity and strips you of the desire to set and accomplish life goals. Hopelessness can cause you to feel as if no efforts are worth it, and in the end, you cannot win. Allow me to share a recent experience that might lend insight to your understanding of how to look at hopelessness differently, and perhaps help you to overcome hopelessness. Here is my second example of a sports experience. Guess you can tell by now I am a fan!

On November 19, 2017 I was watching a Sunday afternoon NFL football game between the Washington Redskins and the New Orleans Saints. It was the fourth quarter and there were less than two minutes on the game clock to play. From where I was sitting, and I am not referring to the seat I was sitting in I am referring to my disposition of mind, all hope of the Saints winning was gone. Oh, come on! You know you would also agree that this team is done, this game is over. It's the fourth quarter, the clock has less than two minutes remaining and the Saints are down by eight points. I thought, there simply is not enough time for this team to come back from an eight-point deficit and win the game.

So, I walked away from the television in preparation to continue on with my day. When all of a sudden, I heard cheering coming from the television, so I zoomed back into the living room to discover that the Saints had scored a touchdown and ultimately the game went into overtime. The Saints experienced the turn of the tide, the tables had turned for them and even I then realized that winning was a real possibility for them at this juncture. Here is my point: what if the Saints held my mindset? Apparently, they did not. They obviously gave no thought to the time clock and what seemed to be unfavorable for them. In their moment of challenge, they possessed a dogged determination, a firm belief, a forceful will, unparalleled skill, and a courageous heart to fight and ultimately defeat their opponent.

This is what you are going to need to defeat depressive thoughts. You will need the tenacity of heart and mind to get you through each self-defeating thought and emotional upset that would otherwise subdue you. Every time you face a fourth quarter experience; and it appears that the clock of your hopefulness is running down, don't lose hope—you will *win*. Make haste to take your eyes off of what is happening against you and know that winning and overcoming is in you, even if you think you need more time than you have in order to overcome.

As the saying goes, "Rome wasn't built in a day." Your best self will not be accomplished in a day. It happens with time. Think about it: do you recall my example of the bridge-building process I mentioned earlier? If you saw the inception of a mighty bridge being built in one month, and the project was completed by the 3rd month; based on what you know about bridges and what it takes for quality, security, safety, durability, would you rush to be the first person to try it out? Anyone who knows me can only imagine the face I'm making right at this moment. Of course, you would not; therefore, do not put so much pressure on yourself to build up your emotionally strong *self*.

Consider the oak tree. It is an old tree. The oak tree is deep, strong, and sturdy. However, the oak tree is as such because of time and experience. The more the wind and elements beat against the oak tree its roots are deepened and strengthened. You are far greater than the most qualified bridge and the oldest, long-standing oak tree. You have what it takes, go for it!

Relationship issues with self, others, and your environment

Experiencing depression can cause your view of self, others, and your environment to be skewed and your outlook will not be good or positive. You might experience low self-esteem and thoughts of unworthiness. Additionally, you might notice you get into more conflict with others than usual or communicate in a short-fused manner. Perhaps you become more cynical and jaded in your comments and responses toward others. There is also the potential to experience increased workplace conflict and/ or dissatisfaction, and also the probability of decreased productivity when you are depressed.

What about difficulty following through with job assignments, frequent tardiness and absenteeism; maybe even quitting multiple jobs? Your family and friends might experience you as agitated, aloof, and pessimistic. Individuals experiencing severe depression sometimes experience relationship issues resulting in breakups and even divorce. In addition, food can lose its savor when you are depressed; and you might find yourself over-indulging and mindlessly eating, but never experiencing satiation.

Low motivation or extreme busyness

When depressed you might experience low motivation,

a lack of energy, fatigue, malaise, and sullenness. These descriptors and many other words generally describe individuals who are dealing with depression. When low in motivation you might feel immobilized and things that once spurred you on cannot do it for you anymore. It is easy to forget what it felt like to be alive and creative when going through depression.

There are times when a lack of motivation can be experienced in one or more than one area of your life. The prognosis is better when there are still some things that you get excited about and things that still motivate, although some things might no longer appeal to you due to depressive symptoms. But be careful, because those things that you still find motivation for can lead to engaging in extreme busyness; which can be counter-productive and prevent you from working on long-term healing. Busyness can serve as a placeholder, a pacifier if-you-will.

Signs that you are becoming extremely busy to cope include but are not limited to constantly being on the go and experiencing increased discomfort with sitting still and relaxing, being busy to cope and avoid dealing with your depressive symptoms might also manifest in pretending to be goal and mission focused, but there is no real point to what you are doing other than to keep busy. Do you experience difficulty prioritizing and balancing your life while in your busyness? If you are more likely to jump to every opportunity to do the next thing, this also could be a sign that you are engaging in non-productive busyness. If you are finding that you are all over the place and you are not allowing for time to center yourself and establish meaningful tasks and goals, you just might be busying yourself to keep from thinking about your depression, all the busy things you engage in might be done so with the hopes to distract from the awful feeling of oppression that is associated with depression.

I get it! I can certainly understand why you would rather be up and about, rather than moping around and feeling sad and sorrowful; and sunken by depression. But if you are not careful to be mindful and self-aware, you could potentially crash and burn.

Suicidal Thoughts and/or Suicide

Unfortunately, suicide is growing more and more to be an outcome of the hopelessness and extreme sadness depression leaves in its wake or course of destruction. When I am working with clients I am careful to remind myself that not all suicidality leads to an attempt. However, if someone contemplates or entertains the idea of suicide repeatedly, the chances of an attempt are more likely to happen. Also, the more individuals attempt suicide, the chances of completing suicide rise by leaps and bounds. Of course, suicide is as a result of hopelessness. When individuals *cannot* see a way out their depression, suicide as an option seems like it is the only viable option to end the hopelessness. In the mind of a deeply depressed person with no good coping skills, suicide is a real answer.

I have heard that people who commit suicide are selfish. The act seems selfish, it seems that the person who commits suicide does not think of anyone but him or herself. There are times when individuals will commit suicide because they see themselves as a problem that needs to be out of the way so others can be happy, such individuals actually believe they are doing everyone a favor through their suicidal act.

Suicide is an indication that such thoughts might exist: nothing else will stop the pain, there is no way that I will ever be happy, my life will always be this way, and so on. Sometimes depressed people really believe that they are a burden to everyone around them. I have asked patients who were suicidal to think of the impact of their actions on those who really care and who would really be destroyed by their act of suicide. A common response was: no one would miss me; the world and my family would be better off without me. As much as suicide might seem like a cry for help or a call for attention, when someone tells you they want to commit suicide; believe them every time. The fact that someone would go to the extreme to bring up the topic of committing suicide speaks volumes that something is going on, even if it is just a cry for help...do something to help!

Poor coping

When in a state of depression individuals generally do not have the ability to engage in effective coping. Effective coping is being able to maintain a positive mindset, engage in emotional intelligence, laugh out loud and laugh often, take initiative to change your situations and circumstances without waiting on standby and allowing others to make decisions over your life, managing your time effectively, and knowing what it means to communicate and problem-solve with yourself and with others. The only way to improve your coping skills is to improve your coping skills. You might have to work diligently to practice and implement these strategies and changes, but it is worth it to overcome your depression.

A lack of effective coping could be as a result of being depressed initially, especially if you experienced depression at a young age in life when developing effective coping was pivotal. Therefore, what can be questioned here is: what came first, the chicken or the egg? Did the depression impact and lead to ineffective coping or did inability to cope lead to depression? This will depend on each specific and unique case and person. For sure, whenever there is a lingering sense or mood of depression, effective coping is not at work. This is not to suggest a person is devoid of any ability to engage in effective coping. However, by and large, effective coping skills are what individuals utilize to deal with life issues and stressors to maintain a sense of well-being and balanced thinking that adds to a positive experience of emotions.

Finally, a huge part of effective coping is being able to give yourself what you need. However, you cannot give yourself what you need if you do not know yourself or have self-awareness. Get to know *you* better. It is not a selfish act to focus on *you*. In fact, I do not know how you can be good for anyone if you do not take moments to pause and take care of *you*. Remember, putting less care into some things does not make you careless; especially if you need to take pause to take good care of yourself.

Hospitalizations

Individuals with prolonged depressive symptoms are at a greater risk for hospitalization for mental, emotional, and medical treatment. Treatment for depression has increased exponentially over the past 30 years and treatment cost has risen by 3 million dollars in the past year. Somatic complaints are often experienced, but without any physical illness as a basis; some such as severe headaches, hypertension, elevated cholesterol, thyroid problems, gastrointestinal complaints, and chronic body pain. Individuals might also experience frequent colds and viruses due to a compromised immune system that is brought on by the stress of depression. If you notice that you are not feeling well physically and there is no medical basis, there might be some emotional upset that is the root cause.

Moreover, depression can lead to the experience of subsequent negative emotions, primarily because attempting to pull one's self out of depression without properly working through the illness can create greater emotional pull and tension in the psyche. Consequently; a snowball of negative, corresponding, emotions are also created. I use this handout, I call The Cycle of Emotions, to help patients identify how one negative emotion quickly leads to another. Especially when individuals do not take the time to understand what is going on inside and utilize moments to get to know themselves better.

Of course, it makes perfect sense to me as to why individuals want to quickly cycle out of negative emotions. Negative emotions do not feel good. To sit in emotional discomfort and feel a sense of hopelessness and helplessness is a bummer, so individuals get busy. Remember the busyness I discussed earlier? People get busy doing something, anything to not feel the pain and discomfort of depression; but busyness does not equal better. Busyness is a Band-Aid. When you do not take necessary steps to address your depressive symptoms adequately, you can spiral downward before you are even aware of what is happening.

Practical solutions are accomplished through your commitment, grit, and tenacity.

CHAPTER 8

LET'S TALK ABOUT HEALTHY

Frequently Asked Questions (FAQs)

> *How do I deal with unrealistic*
> *expectations and perfectionism?*

The first thing to do is understand how you think about your thoughts regarding unrealistic expectations and perfectionism. This might be most effectively accomplished through reflection, meditation, and journal writing. Once you have developed insight, you can begin to work through your challenges by focusing more on what is effective and less on what is right. What is right or not right is yours to decide and the definition of a right or wrong way to do something is going to vary from person-to-person; for this reason, it is important to focus on effectiveness, and not so much perfectionism.

I usually have a hard time feeling like I'm
good enough. How can I shake this?

Perhaps now is a good time to redefine what good enough is. At some point, throughout your life journey, you learned how to think about what it means to be "good enough." You can rewrite your script and however you define good enough, then that is what good enough is to you. Oftentimes individuals have a difficult time allowing themselves to change what they have learned over time. You must begin to give yourself permission to think for yourself.

The only way to add power and strength to your mind is to work it like a muscle until you build it up. This means practicing new ways of thinking, surrounding yourself with healthy-thinking people, immersing your thoughts in healthy reading material, and listening to inspiring messages by motivating individuals. Develop a mantra that works for you and rehearse it to yourself daily; frame it and keep it before you if you must. If you keep at it, you are bound to notice changes; even if the changes are small and subtle at first. The better you begin to feel, the better you will desire to feel.

How can I overcome my inner critic that
keeps reminding me of past mistakes?

The tricky thing about our resourceful brain is that

it allows us to remember. You will never, ever forget life events unless you lose your memory. Not all of your life memories will always be at the forefront of your thinking, but memories do come to the fore. When negative, self-defeating thoughts emerge, you want to first ask yourself; "why is this coming up for me, and why now?" There might be something to glean from by slowing down your thought processes to understand what is happening in those moments when your past comes back to haunt you. Maybe there are unresolved matters surrounding a recurring event that continues to be replayed in your head. Perhaps you might need to forgive yourself and/or someone else related to a particular matter. It might be worth it to you to do some exploring, and it might be helpful to explore with a trusted friend or professional.

My family of origin is a mess, and although I try to become disentangled, I keep being pulled back into family drama. What can I do to remain focused and set healthy boundaries without feeling like I am dissing my family?

Separation and individuation is a part of the human developmental process that is necessary for healthy growth and development. During this process, you learn who you are apart from others. You tap into your own unique qualities and you begin to discover what you like based on your own personality. You continue to grow and develop throughout life and there comes a time for some individuals when things about their family are things they do not want to be a part of any longer.

This does nothing to the family tie, you are family

regardless; but it might be difficult to socialize and enjoy certain things you once enjoyed together. This is not a matter of right or wrong, unless you deem it so. This could simply be a time in your life when you need and desire something different, by virtue of the path and course your life has taken. We all grow and develop differently and at different times. There is a way to continue to enjoy your family by engaging in things you do have in common.

Feeling like a loner in a family system that does not seem to desire change is a common issue I have dealt with as a practitioner, if each family member can respect each other's path and not try to change or control others; you can continue on your desired path and still enjoy aspects of your family. If your family discourages you and does not celebrate your desired change, this is when you have to decide how you will develop healthy boundaries. Remember this: you are only responsible for how you communicate effectively, you are not responsible for how your family responds.

I notice that it is easy for people to make me feel guilty when I don't do things they want me to do, and then I get upset and angry for feeling used and underappreciated, so why do I keep giving in?

The word guilty is a legal term, and you have committed no crime by declining to do what others want you to do. Also, no one has the power to make you feel anything. How you feel is an automatic reaction following your thinking about a given event. For example, if you are asked to babysit your sibling's child and you are tired from working all week; but you say yes so you won't feel guilty if you say no. The first thing you want to ask yourself is: why do I feel guilty for wanting to take care of myself after working all week long?

Oftentimes, other individuals in this same position will tell me that they do not want to seem mean or hurt someone's feelings. I generally reply: you cannot know if someone's feelings will be hurt and you cannot control another's reaction. I then ask: do you feel hurt when someone says no to you? More often than not the reply is—yes! In this example, hard decisions must be made. It takes time to learn to feel emotionally comfortable about something that has caused such emotional discomfort for some time.

The only way to conquer this fear is to start somewhere. People might not like it, and let's be honest; some people might disconnect from you. If this should happen, then you will know that your connection was built on an unstable foundation. When someone walks out of your life because of what you will not do for them, this is a form of control, and unfortunately sometimes there is usury involved.

Consider This...

In order to reach your goal of attaining a sense of self you can enjoy, and in order to overcome depression, you will need something other than *you*. You will need Motivation, Manpower, Maturity and Management Ability, and More...

Motivation

Motivation is your enthusiasm, determination, drive, and initiative. Motivation can be internal, external, or both.

Manpower

Manpower, is that power available to you by another or others, for the purpose of getting something done.

Maturity and Management Ability

Maturity and Management Ability involves insight, good judgment, and thought processes that are logical, coherent, and goal-focused.

And More....

The *more* you will need depends on *you*. You are uniquely created and crafted; therefore, what you need will be specific to you. "The *more* you might need could manifest in the need for more energy, effort, time, and so on. Note, as you read earlier on in this reading, change costs something. However, remember to steer clear from the comparison game, while on your journey to emotional wholeness. No two people need the same thing, and if they do, there could be varying degrees in which more is needed.

Additionally, you will find that there are different levels of maturity, motivation, and also differences in access to manpower or the quality and kind of manpower. So, don't compare!

Your Thought Life Matters

Make it a habit of becoming a person of query. I ask more questions now than I have ever asked in my life. Not necessarily questions toward others. I ask myself questions. One thing I learned in grade school that I will never forget. One of my teachers said to the class: "the dumbest question is the one you don't ask." Here is what I consider a comical account of something I queried recently. The older I get the more difficult it is for me to just let some things slide without asking why. So, I was watching this Domino's Pizza commercial during 2017 Christmas holiday season. The man in the commercial pulled up to his driveway and a large tree fell on top of his SUV and from all appearances smashed the vehicle to the point of being totaled. The man opened his car door and frantically awaited to see if the pizza was still edible. Once he opened the box and saw what was advertised as a piping hot pizza, unscathed by the tree accident, he sighed in relief and proceeded to go inside. As he walked onto the snowy ground he slipped, the pizza came out of the box, went into the air, and fell onto the snow.

The next scene of the commercial shows the man in Domino's store getting another pizza. You see, the advertisement was actually about how you can get a free replacement pizza if your pizza is somehow destroyed after leaving the store. So, I wondered. Number 1, with a seemingly totaled car, why is the pizza the most important thing. Number 2, there were no other vehicles in sight, so how did the man get back to Domino's. Did he ask a neighbor, take a taxi or Uber? I don't know, but these are some questions that ran through my mind. Sort of like

Arsenio Hall, the man who coined the statement: things that make you go hmmmm?

Of course, the commercial was funny and I totally get what Domino's was advertising for. I used this example to illustrate how I have gotten so much into query that sometimes I query even the littlest things that baffle me. Why, you might ask, would I waste my time on what seems to be trivial thinking?

In the grand scheme of things this commercial example is no big deal, right? Well, it is not so much about the commercial, but my illustration of how important it is to pay attention to those things we might miss because we get caught up in other details, maybe even things that are distracting. A lot of what is experienced by way of depression is experienced because of what we allow in our thoughts that impact our emotions. However, depression is not only caused by what we allow in our thoughts, but depression is caused by what we continue to tolerate that is not helpful or useful, because we are distracted for so long. When we finally look up. Depression is there.

Now, the Domino's commercial might not be something you would pay attention to, it's all for advertisement and laughs, of course; and this example is not to criticize or be petty. My aim is to point out how important observation can be in more serious situations, and illustrate how much you can miss along the way if you do not pay careful attention as needed. You know, that job you took without critically examining, or the person you married, and the second person you married, the relationship you tolerated, the abuse you took for too long, the house or car you purchased, that investment you made too hastily, and the money you overspend. All these things can add to your depressed mood. Especially if trails of regret, resentment, shame, guilt, disappointment, and setbacks follow. You will do well to get into the habit of critical examination of important behaviors within you and around you. There are times when critical examination is important and when you do not engage in critical examination of information and critical examination of people you embrace, this can ultimately become emotionally costly to you.

It took me a while to feel comfortable with asking questions to others, but now I am proficient at asking questions in general. So, why is query important as related to depression? Because depression is as a result of the way events are interpreted. Your thoughts matter. If you can change the way you think you can improve your emotional state and possibly prevent a persistent depressed mood. Also, what you entertain can have an impact on your mood. This is why it is important to develop self-awareness of what you need, and commit yourself to giving yourself what you need to be in your best mood. We are very sensual beings. Later on, in this reading, I will provide tools on how to gain awareness of how to use your senses to improve thoughts, emotions, and mood; and address and manage depression.

Speaking of sensual, a pertinent example comes to mind as I reflect on an experience in my Psychopharmacology course. My professor presented a study related to the brain and how music impacts the brain and mood. The study involved an individual who had been prescribed pain killers and sedatives. One day, while listening to heavy metal music, the subject took medication in excess. The study focused on the heavy metal music and its impact on the brain, to cause irresponsible, impulsive behavior. In a euphoric state, while listening to heavy metal music, the individual ended up overdosing. The conclusion was that the music, which was the only thing done differently, impacted the subject's usual behavioral pattern as related to the overdose.

As I am writing, I began to think about the impact of music on the brain from a personal standpoint. I think about how emotions and moods can shift in a moment depending on what is entertained. Let's review some music samples together, I have added a few lines from the following song titles: *Hopeless, Love On the Brain, Through the Fire, I'm Going Down, You're Gonna Love Me, Keeping a Light, Memory Lane, I Tried, I Found Love on a Two-Way Street, Cause I Love You, Going in Circles, It's You That I Need, You Got Your Hooks In Me, Piece of My Love, The Weekend, No Love, and I am Nothing Without You.*

Just glancing at the song titles, I cannot help but feel the strong sense of hopelessness and desperation that these lyrics consist of. For some, these are songs that are enjoyed and might have no emotional impact; perhaps you cannot relate at all. However, there are others who would say these titles and lyrics profoundly speak their experiences.

Hopeless… Dionne Farris
They say I'm hopeless,
As a penny with a hole in it.
They say I'm no less,
Than up to my head in it.

Love on the Brain... Rihanna
And I'll run for miles just to get a taste.
Must be love on the brain.
It beats me black and blue.
But I can't get enough.

Through The Fire... Chaka Khan
Through the fire,
To the limit, to the wall.
For a chance to be with you,
I'd gladly risk it all.

I cannot resist this insertion: When she says: "risk it all," exactly what does she mean? I suspect there would be a cutoff point to risk-taking. But when entrenched and entangled in matters of the heart and soul, sometimes chances are taken, even to the point of risking it all. I will be real transparent and honest here, I have lived long enough to admit that I have taken some risks, and possibly "risked it all," without realizing; but I can assure you, I would never intentionally sign up for risking it all, it's definitely not in my DNA.

This might be a true statement for you as well. Hey, let's be real! There are times when certain decisions are made when we are not in a good place emotionally; yes, during times of depression. But sometimes we can find a way to turn our depression into laughter, especially when we are able to reflect and see how far we have come. However, if you are still struggling as you read this book, no worries; help has come to the rescue. Today is the day that you can say "no more" to living dangerously, going through the fire of depressive thoughts and emotions, and risking it all. Today is the day you begin to laugh. Let's continue:

I'm Going Down... Rose Royce (also Mary J. Blige)
I'm going down.
I'm going down.
'Cause you ain't around, baby.
My whole world's upside down.

You're Gonna Love Me, by Jennifer Holiday
(also Jennifer Hudson)
And I am telling you,
I'm not going.
You're the best man I'll ever know.
There's no way I can ever go.

Keeping a Light...Natalie Cole
I'm keeping a light shining in the window,
Just in case he decides to come home.
He's a beautiful man, kinda hard to understand but,
He's the only good man that I know.

Memory Lane...Minnie Riperton
Be still my foolish heart.
Don't let this feeling start.
Back down memory lane.
I don't want to go... save me save me.

I Tried... Angela Bofill
I tried to do the best I can for you,
But it seems it's not enough.
And you know I care, even when you're not there.
But it's not what you want.

I Found Love on a Two-Way Street... Stacy Lattisaw
I found love on a two way street and lost it on a lonely
highway.
Love on a two way street and lost it on a lonely highway.

HERE IS SOMETHING FOR THE MEN.
I'M AN EQUAL OPPORTUNITY
KIND OF A GIRL

Cause I love you... Lenny Williams
One time things got so bad until,
I had to go to one of my friends and talk to him.
And then it got so bad, it got so bad,
Till one time I thought I'd roll myself up in a big old ball
and die.

Going In Circles... *Friends of Distinction*
You got me going in circles (oh round and round I go).
You got me going in circles.
(Oh round and round I go, I'm spun out over you).
I'm a faceless clock, with timeless hopes that never stop.

It's You That I Need... *Enchantment*
Something strange is happening.
You don't belong to me anymore it seems.
I'm all alone in my dreams, yeah.
I just feel so weak.

You Got Your Hooks In Me... *The O'Jays*
Oh, oh, baby, I guess you've got your hooks in me.
And I walk like a fish.
And, baby, I just can't break free.
You know this thing is killin' me.

Piece of My Love... *En-vogue (also Guy)*
You can have a piece of my love.
It's waiting for you.
Girl, it's true (I do love you).

Finally, for the millennial readers...

SZA...The weekend
Tuesday and Wednesday, Thursday and Friday,
I just keep him satisfied through the weekend.
You're like 9 to 5, I'm the weekend.

No Love...August Alsina and Nicki Minaj
Believe we had a great night but I ain't the type to tell you
that I miss you,
Let's just party till we can't, ain't no loving me.
And I'm the one to blame, ain't no loving me.
So don't come looking for love.

One day I tested myself for a real-life experience. I played the most upbeat, hip-hop, rap song I could find on YouTube and of course, I danced and did the whole sing-along thing as well. I was feeling quite excited and euphoric, it was as if I was on cloud 9, so-to-speak. After the song ended, I continued with the process and found one of those good old love songs, one with real deep, lyrical meaning. So, I listened to:

I Am Nothing Without You... Whitney Houston
Stay in my arms if you dare,
Or must I imagine you there.
Don't walk away from me.
I am nothing if I don't have you.

A sad experience happened quickly for me. Before I knew it my energy fizzled, my eyes watered, I was no longer happy; and guess what? If you take yourself through this test of listening to music that impact your memory in a saddening manner; and you allow this music to impact your thoughts and ultimately your emotions, you are going to end up how? You got it…. you are going to end up feeling sad and depressed! Even if only for a moment. I would ask, why would you do this to yourself?

I trust that you have enjoyed this trip down memory lane, for some; and an introduction for others. I also trust that my point was well-received. If you are going to experience improved emotions and mood, you will need to monitor your intake. As I stated, you are sensually connected to yourself, others, and this world; so stay aware. Check your emotional temperature regularly. If you find you are in a bad place emotionally, do not just sit there aimlessly.

Should you decide to process to determine what is going on with you, do so effectively and intentionally. Have someone process with you if you can find a trusting friend or professional, but by all means; do not ignore warning signs that you could be headed to a depressive state of mind.

Your Inner Feng Shui

If you will experience real, lasting change; change will begin from within. Because change has to begin from within, you can benefit from the following concepts to build yourself anew from the inside, beginning with the way you think.

Practice metacognition

Metacognition is engaging in thought processes in such a way that you actually think about what you think about. Once you realize thoughts that you typically allow to remain, then you take yourself through the process of weeding out what thoughts are worthy to remain. If you deem certain thoughts as worthy to remain, have a good plan for what you will do with those thoughts. For example, if you decide that it is worth it to allow thoughts of an old relationship to remain, how will you effectively think about these thoughts? What is your goal for allowing these thoughts? Is there unfinished business in your psyche and emotions that are needful to work through?

Next, you take yourself through the process of examining the way you think about your thoughts. At this point, you critically examine your thoughts for evidence that what you are thinking about your thoughts is rational. For example, if you have a thought that it is not worth it to you to keep trying to get a promotion or start-up a small business; you might ask yourself: where is the supporting evidence that it is not worth it? Continuing to engage in this type of critical examination of your thoughts can help you to narrow down your thoughts to a more rational and less emotional conclusion.

Reconstruct your negative mindset

It is necessary for me to highlight the difficulty of effective critical examination of your thoughts when you are prone to a negative mindset. A negative mindset is simply a mind that is firm and set in a negative position. When this is the case, it can be difficult, but not impossible, to effectively critically examine your thoughts. Your negative mindset will always present evidence that might seem to be a plausible reason to lean more toward a negativistic possibility or outcome. For example, going back to the aforementioned example; you might ask yourself, where is the evidence that it is not worth it for you to keep trying to get a promotion or start-up a small business? Your mindset might accurately say the following: there are others more qualified for the promotion, I have no entrepreneurs in my family, I do not know the first thing about being a business owner, and so forth. The reason that you buy into these thoughts is because these thoughts might be true. This is when it will benefit you to continue with metacognition processing, think about what you are thinking about and how you are thinking about what you are thinking about.

At this point, you can validate that it is true that there are others more qualified for the promotion, you have no entrepreneurs in your family, you do not know the first thing about being a business owner, etc. Then you can say; however, there might be different qualities about myself as a person that might be more needful, it is never too late to learn, I can become the first entrepreneur in my family, and I will never know if I do not try. You can also do a cost/benefits analysis and ask yourself what will it cost you to try and what might it benefit you to try?

Embrace will power

As you challenge yourself to forcefully deal with your negative mindset, you can get more in touch with your positive will power. According to a human development theory, by psychoanalyst Erik Erikson, the will is developed during ages 2-3 of the stages of human development. Will power is in you, even when you do not feel like you have the energy or courage to embrace and implement your will power. As stated earlier, you will have to muscle your way, mentally and emotionally, through some of your thoughts that hinder you. If you keep at it, and if you align yourself with people of a like mindset of courage and strength, and if you gather as many resources as you can to overcome depressive and defeating thoughts; you can feel yourself breaking through barriers that once seemed impenetrable.

Reconsider your goals

There are times when revising life goals might be necessary. In fact, reconsidering and revising life goals, if thought out carefully, can give you a much-needed boost and inspiration to forge out a path that is remarkable. Being able to imagine something different, other than what you have routinely experienced, might just be the lift you need to improve your emotions and mood.

Discover your keys to inner peace

What brings you peace? Have you forgotten what a peaceful life feels like? Have you ever known peace? Have you become inundated and overwhelmed with life and somehow the idea of inner peace seems so foreign and unfamiliar that you cannot imagine it? Here are some tips: *create a vision, help others, challenge yourself, confront your fears, rewrite your story, identify a positive support network, talk it out, and journal your journey.*

Create a vision

In your mind there is an image, a picture of what life can be like; and oh, how liberating it can be when the mind is free to imagine and create a vision of possibility. However, depression will keep you from being able to see with your mind's eye. You might ask, do I have to wait until my depression lifts before I can see, imagine, and create a vision. Absolutely not! You might have to exert extra effort, but you can get yourself to a place where you become astute at exercising the mind and using your mind to hurdle over matters that keep you weighed down. Remember, one way to do so is to practice *metacognition*.

Help others along your journey to a more peaceful you

Although it might not seem the best recommendation, especially when you are already feeling subdued, helping others and focusing on the struggles of others can help you realize that you are not alone. I am not at all suggesting that you take advantage of utilizing someone's pain to take your mind off of your own pain. What I am stating is this: we all share in a common struggle of managing life, in various kinds and contexts. Since, according to John Donne, "No man is an island entire of itself," it is befitting for me to point out the benefit that can be found when you share in another's struggles and pains. A sort of a parallel-processing can occur; you might be surprised that when you are sincerely present and genuinely engaging in someone's struggles, you might feel better simultaneously.

Challenge yourself

Believing in your possibility to overcome depression is the first step to challenging yourself to overcome depression. I say believing is the first step because there are times when your belief is all you will have. The odds seem to be against you and you cannot imagine better days. So believe even when you cannot see it, believe until you see it. During these times it is good to say to yourself: Although I cannot see it, I believe better is possible.

It is also at this point that you can benefit from stating

and restating, and declaring your depression-free life; you will keep at it until you are depression-free. You do not simply want to learn to live with depression do you? Of course not, if depression-free is a possibility, then this is what you are signing up for. Rely on positive surroundings, good, wholesome people, encouraging literature and quotes, and any and all healthy resources you can access.

Confront your fears

It is important for me to discuss the fear factor. Depending on how long you have been dealing with depression, living without what has been your norm for some time could be challenging and could create fear. You might ask: how do I live depression-free after being depressed so long? You might also fear becoming depression-free and then relapsing back into that dark place. You might wonder how others will respond to you and how you will feel practicing principles of empowerment, initiative, and assertiveness now that you are depression-free. So, I certainly understand there might be fear, but confront your fears until you are fearful no longer.

Rewrite your story

Now is the time to tell a new story. Regardless of where you are in the stages of change, you can begin to rewrite. Let's say you are in the contemplative phase of the stages of change. Begin rewriting there. Everything that you have to say about your journey is valuable, important, and grist for the mill as you make progress. Let's say you are in the practicing phase of the stages of change, still some fear? It's okay, keep at it; you're doing great! For some, you are no longer plagued with depression. Life is better, roses smell sweeter, music is joyful noise again, conversation and communication with others have meaning again, you are in touch with many aspects of *self,* aspects that depression stole from you. You have something to say that not only others need to hear, but you need to hear what you have to say about you, reverberating in your ears and in your mind. Become your biggest fan and cheerleader. It is not selfish to do so, it is needful to do so. It is needful so that you always remember what you need to do for *self,* so that you can minimize the likelihood of going back to that dark place, a sunken place. Does this mean depressive moments will not strike again; of course not, feeling depressed is a part of being alive. However, to minimize a prolonged depressed mood, you now have tools to implement. You have learned information that you cannot unknow. You are armed with an arsenal of weaponry to aid you as you navigate through life and manage life in such a way that you are not controlled and subdued by depression. *Sing out loud, and dance (get moving and create dynamic energy).* I like this particular line of the lyrics to a song by Drake, Drake says: "you showing off, but it's alright; it's a short life." When you have been deep in depression for such a long and enduring time, and you feel the liberty once you are unshackled; you realize how short life really can be. So yeah, show off the new you, it's a short life!

Identify a positive support network

Have you seen the capital one commercial: what's in your wallet? Have you seen the American express commercial, don't leave home without it? Well, I challenge you today: who's in your support network? What's in your support toolbox? The moment a crisis hits is not the time to try to scram and determine what your defense team is comprised of. Be sure to have people around you who can be a strong line of defense for you. These people will know and understand you. They will give you good advice, feedback, and support. These people are also healthy to be in relationship with and they are not toxic. Think about it. In the NFL there is an offensive line and a defensive line. The defensive line is designed to stop any plans on the opposing offensive team. Of course, the opposing team has plans to win, but the defensive line on the opposite team is to make sure their opponent's plans are blocked. Depression wins when you are not suited and ready with a defensive plan.

You have just read why it is important to have a good defensive line. However, a part of what it means to be ready is to also have a good offensive line. This means what? This means that everyday your feet hit the floor there is a plan in place to win. You are feeling good and ready to face the day because you slept and rested well, you have a healthy breakfast prepared, you have your day organized in such a way that you can minimize stress that leads to depressive symptom, as best as you can. You did not awaken to bings and pings on your electronic devices. You did not engage in social media drama. You stated a positive affirmation to yourself, perhaps even reached out to someone to give a word of encouragement. If you are spiritual, perhaps you prayed for guidance, meditated, and engaged in motivational literature.

This is what a good offensive plan looks like. A good offensive plan is needful because life, the job, the world, traffic, parenting, the spouse, and even *you,* can get in the way at any given moment and disrupt your feel-good vibe.

Talk it out

Now that you have your support network and your plans set in place so that you can succeed, think about what it means to talk it out. Speak about your success. Speak as an expert. You have gone through and you have come through, and someone can benefit from knowing that overcoming depression is possible. I am aware that some people are private and shy to share their personal experiences. But, someone's life might be saved by your story.

Keep a journal

A keep sake or memoir of your experiences can serve as a reference for you and for others. Although there might be some things that you want to forget and never go back and face again, leave it to your own discretion. You know what will and will not work for you. Only when you find it helpful, allow your journey to serve as a source of accomplishment. A reminder of your courage, willingness, and stick-to-itiveness that has led to your triumphant victory.

Your Outer Feng Shui

Consists of your connectedness to your senses, such as:

Colors and lighting you see

You might be surprised how colors and lights can be avenues by which you take in matter that impacts you internally. Artwork and certain lighting styles, colors, and watts can create a mood change. Additionally, you might consider getting involved in an art class, being creative if-you-will. An alternative is to set up an easel in your home. Coloring books and water paint from the dollar store can be simple enough, yet very helpful in improving your outer feng shui.

Sounds you hear

Earlier on in this reading, I wrote, at length, about the impact of music on the brain. In keeping with what I have already presented, I will remain in that vein of thought and highlight other such sounds as birds chirping, and taking time to listen for the sound of the wind blowing on a breezy day. Also, going near a lake to hear the waters can provide you with an external experience and improve your mood. Moreover, you can find downloads and relaxation sounds to calm your mind so that you can clear some of your mental clutter and think rationally.

Scents you smell

I cannot say enough about the way smells can improve your mood. Your scent intake can range from essential oils, to scent of flowers, or baked goods, perfumes and colognes, candles, perfumed incense, scented plug-ins, and so much more. Whatever you are not allergic to, go ahead and give it a try.

Delicacies you taste

Taste can also be a huge factor in experiencing a change in your mood. Generally, you know what those items are that you taste and you consider them your comfort foods. Whether it is an actual food item, a snack, ice cream, and yes; junk food. Whatever "your thing is," you know it. You have tried and tested it, and it has proven effective. However, you want to be sure that you are not relying on unhealthy items. These choices can be temporary fixes, but can also prove counterproductive in the long-run.

Positive people you touch and embrace

Of course, touch is very significant to overall health and feelings of well-being. Nevertheless, I do respect that there are some people who minimally desire touch, and some do not want to be touched at all. I understand there are various reasons that this is so, and I actually wrote about this topic, briefly, in my book on *communication*. But, do you remember earlier when I wrote a quote that no man is an island? This is what I mean by the importance of touch. For example, you might try a hug for those who are saddened, a touch on the shoulder to demonstrate concern and understanding, a shoulder to cry on, a handshake to greet or congratulate, a high-five, a chest-bump, a fist-bump, and so many more ways of touch and human contact that can make a difference in one's mood. I dare not leave out physical intimacy (and everything that goes along with it). However, it is important to note that physical intimacy is never a cure for depression. It can help when experienced appropriately.

TRY THIS

Process of Attrition

Take a moment for this exercise. Prepare yourself. You will need a rubberband in hand; that's it. Select a fairly thick rubberband, but not too thick. You will need to be able to stretch it, but not break it easily. Once you have your rubberband in hand, cut it once to be able to extend it between both hands. Hold one end with your left hand using your index finger and your thumb. Repeat this process with the right hand, hold the other end of the rubberband between your right index finger and your thumb. Now, begin to tug gently with both hands, stretching the rubberband. Stretch the rubberband until you feel the tension between both hands. The more you tug, the more tension you should feel. Remember, do not tug to the point of breaking the rubberband.

Now, imagine that your left hand represents your depressive symptoms: your sadness, fear, hurt, fatigue, lack of motivation and pleasure, anger, agitation, insomnia or hypersomnia, and so on. Now, also imagine that at some point you have reached out to find support, and gain insight and tools to overcome your depression. The end of the rubberband that you hold with your right hand represents your strengths and your new insights, and your tools and strategies to overcome depressive thoughts.

As you tug with both your left and right hand you now realize what is happening. Your depression is pulling you in one direction and your tools and strategies are pulling you in another direction. This external example is a representation of your internal struggle, as related to depression. Your right hand pulls you toward healing, and all of your negative experiences, thoughts, and emotions propel you to remain stuck. You feel tension from both realms as the pulling continues. This same tension is experienced in your psyche as you learn new ways of thinking and emoting, but those old depressive ways and patterns of thinking continue to fight for your attention. You are left feeling drained and frazzled, but as you work through issues and events what you will notice is this: you will notice that the tension from your depression and dysthymia will lift and lessen. This will only happen as you strengthen your euthymic end and implement and reinforce your tools and strategies. Hopefully you did not let that rubberband go; but if you have let it go, get back to your holding position and tug again with both hands.

At this time, I want you to slowly release the tension by bringing your hands toward each other. In this portion of the exercise you are integrating both parts. What does this mean for your psyche and your emotions you ask? This means that you are releasing tension so that you bring your understanding of depression to the point of recognizing what to do about your depression. When you are able to do this effectively your thoughts become integrated, you are no longer frazzled and fearful of depression, and tension in your psyche can released.

Be careful and patient; however, because when you try to force yourself too quickly toward a resolve and toward a happier you, your efforts can become counterproductive. If you are pushing yourself harder than you are mentally and emotionally ready to heal, you can become more frustrated and agitated, this can lead to anxiety, and ultimately more frustration, sadness, and back to depression again. So, relax and release the tension by gently applying strategies daily, like you apply ointment to a sore spot. You apply daily; throughout the day, and voila! You notice the sore spot has improved. Likewise, keep at applying strategies, staying connected with an emotionally and mentally healthy support system, and take good care of yourself inside and out.

What Shape Are You In?

I am not referring to your physical health, although your physical health is important to your overall well-being. I am referring to you as a whole. What are your strengths, habits, attitudes, plans/partnerships, and energies?

Strengths

Self-awareness is necessary to know your strengths. I am sure you can think of areas in your life and identify your strong-points. Although, it seems to be human nature to either overestimate or underestimate our strengths. Be realistic, have a healthy perspective on what your strengths are and keep them in view; utilize those strengths as a springboard to continue improving your shape.

Habits

What are your life habits that are working for you and what are some life habits that work against you? Take a moment to reflect and journal, you will need this insight to help with careful planning and restructuring your life so that you can minimize stressful habits that can lead to depression. Remember, any habits that are not adding to your life fulfillment and satisfaction, are subtracting from it, and sometimes you have to divide and conquer in order to multiply and maximize your life; it's simple mathematics!

Attitudes

I heard this statement a lot growing up: "your attitude determines your altitude." I agree. Attitudes that flow from a healthy thought life can propel you onward and upward. Throughout this reading, you will be reminded of the correlation between your thoughts, emotions, mood, and behavioral response to yourself, others, and life in general. How you think in a given moment can create a positive or negative emotion, try shifting your thoughts and you might be amazed at how your emotions shift. It is often said that we should not trust our emotions because our emotions change constantly. Our emotions change constantly because we shift our mind so often. A solid mindset about your strengths can help you develop improved attitudes and healthy habits.

Plans and Partnerships

Now that you have considered your strengths and identified healthy habits and attitudes; you can plan effectively and build healthy partnerships for your life goals. You see, when you are depressed it is difficult to be decisive and it certainly is difficult to form healthy partnerships. You might begin by taking this trifecta of understanding into consideration: capable, willable, and desirable. When it comes down to planning and healthy partnerships, what are you capable of doing at this juncture? Also, consider whether or not you are willing to do what you are capable of doing, and finally; is what you are capable and willing to do, also what is desirable for you to do? These three are interlinked and are also necessary for planning forward and establishing healthy partnerships.

Energies

Now your positive energies can flow! You are thinking in a healthy manner, you are realistic about *you*, and you are strong enough to make continued decisions that add to your feelings of well-being. You are surrounding yourself with positively charged people; the energy and synergy of your positive surroundings continually add to the person you are reconstructing.

What to Do...

1. *Identify antidotes that lead to a locus of self-worth discovery*

Fighting through negative thoughts can be a very arduous task. So much so that you might want to give up and throw in the towel. But don't! Keep training yourself to carve out different thought processes until you have identified remedies that get you to discovering your self-worth. The worth is there, you just have to connect with it. View retrospectively, introspectively, and circumspectly. In doing so, you will experience an understanding of how you are wired based on your past, you will also understand how you are internally wired when you introspect, and when you view yourself circumspectly, you are viewing yourself through eyes of wisdom and carefulness.

2. *Understand earlier attachments and how they correlate to self-loathing and negative self-dialogue*

It is important to understand how you have come to think the way you think. From earlier attachments in life, you were thought how to perceive and how to process information. Your lenses matter. For example, If I ask you to put on a pair of sunglasses with pink lenses and I put on a pair of sunglasses with purple lenses; what is in front of you will appear pink in color and what is in front of me will appear purple in color. We might both be looking at the same item, but the color of the lenses we look through will cause us to see the same items colored differently.

Your lenses color, form, and inform your experiences. And then one day you begin to feel down and depressed because your life view is no longer working for you. You are now growing, morphing, and developing into something other than who you once were. Growth and development is always a painful process, but a very worthwhile process once you are face-to-face with the results.

3. *Rewire your mind*

Understand your life story, embrace it, and rewrite it. If you always do what you have always done you will always get what you have always gotten. Breaking away from old ways of thinking can be challenging, as I have already mentioned; but overcoming challenges is a very real possibility. Utilize self-help reading material, link up with a counselor/therapist, and any other necessary resources that might help you reach your goals.

4. *Don't compare*

You are uniquely you, I cannot express this enough. With this thought in mind, steer clear of the comparison game. I understand that as you are developing, social comparison is what happens; but you can work to eventually deal with comparison in a healthy way. Especially when it impairs your forward mobility and keeps you looking at the next person or the next thing. Here is an example that you might find helpful and I'll let you have it at no cost. There is a distinct difference between a lemon cake and a chocolate cake. A couple of feature differences are apparent for sure. You can notice the difference by the way the cakes look and smell. So, if you prefer one over the other, there is no comparison.

Now let's say you only like chocolate cake. You might say: there are all different kinds of chocolate cakes such as dark chocolate, milk chocolate, german chocolate, etc. This is a true statement. You decide you want a milk chocolate cake. You show up at the bakery and discover there are 3 milk chocolate cakes baked by 3 different bakers. This could make your choice difficult. My point you ask? We all have differences and similarities, and who you uniquely are is useful. The goal is to be the best *you* that you can be. Let your worth shine forth and you will be amazed at the positivity you elicit. Don't get caught up in the comparison shenanigans.

H- A- L-T

This acronym is used in alcoholics anonymous (AA) to help individuals with awareness regarding lifestyle choices that could potentially lead to relapse. Individuals are encouraged to "halt," to pay attention and engage in mindfulness, to avoid potential stress that might lead to relapse.

A timely example of mindfulness presents at this present moment as I am writing. I have taken an assignment to respond to a critical incident at the Ritz Carlton Hotel in downtown Dallas. Seated in the red room at the Ritz Carlton Hotel in downtown Dallas, I am writing in between consulting. After stepping away for a moment to walk and stretch my legs, I returned and noticed beautiful melody above my head. The music playing from the wall speakers is soothing and noticeable, but was not so before. I thought, hmmm...was this music playing all along and I did not hear it due to the ongoing noise in my head? I suspect the music had been on and I just noticed because my mind is open and receptive now that I am taking a break. Hence my point, mindfulness is necessary and it affords opportunities to notice many things that are going on around you that you might miss due to being too distracted and too busy. Back to *HALT*.

Alcoholics anonymous (AA) teaches individuals to learn what to do when *hungry, angry, lonely, and tired.* I too have taken the "halt" position to teach you how to address certain behaviors that lead to stress and ultimately depression. The wording has been changed a bit, as befitting for the context of this writing.

Know what to do when you become too hurried, agitated, lonely, or tired:

Hurried

When you are too much in a hurry you can miss out on a lot of important things in life. Take your time. Of course, there are times in life when time is of the essence; whether it is due to poor time management or due to unforeseen circumstances that put you in a bind and forces hurriedness. However, do your best to plan well and manage time effectively to minimize the possibility of hurriedness.

Here is an example of what I mean when I say you can miss out on a lot being in a hurry. Think of travel, if-you-will. If you choose to travel by plane, for sure you will get to your destination much more quickly than if you were driving, that is if all goes well with your flight. However, when you are in the air there are lots of things, places, and scenery that you miss out on. When you are driving, or when you are on a bus or train, you are at a much slower pace; but, you get to experience and take in so much more. With ground travel, you get to stop and smell the roses, should you decide. You get to take up-close photos of places and things to serve as memoirs of your journey. Consider it or not, but these moments are all a part of your life experiences. So, remember, don't be too hurried!

Agitated

Life will invariably present opportunities for agitation to arise. There are times when you absolutely cannot foresee agitation coming on, and before you know it you are deep in agitation. Reflect back on the previous point about being hurried, can you imagine how hurriedness can lead to agitation? It certainly can. Make it your goal to live a well-balanced stress-less life. You will never be free of stress, as life is filled with good and bad stress. But you can live a life of less stress when you take the time to plan and manage your life and relationships.

Lonely

Loneliness can be a real trigger that can lead to depression. Oftentimes, you might not realize that the well of your life is empty due to being lonely. Humans are not meant to be without relationships of some sort. If you are not in a significant relationship, if you live alone; keep something alive around you. If it is plants, goldfish, a pet; whatever it is, life around you can make a difference. Just note: healthy relationships are what you will need in order to minimize stress that can lead to depression. If you are engaging in toxic relationships, your well will be drained of the freshness and vitality you need to experience well-being.

Tired

Being too tired can also be draining. Get proper rest and relaxation. Good sleep hygiene is vital to your overall well-being and functioning, but relaxation is important as well. During your awake moments, be sure that you know what to do to relax yourself. Engage all of your senses and taste healthy and tasty snacks, breathe into your nostrils, scents that are calming, listen to something soothing or comical (get a good belly laugh), handle what feels relaxing to touch; and finally, focus your gaze on scenery, or pics, or images that are lighthearted and add to your smile.

And whatever you do, STOP protesting your current situation. STOP saying that this or that should not be happening. Unfortunately it is happening, but it does not have to continue. Your situation is what it is for many reasons I'm sure. Protesting will not help you, it will only frustrate you. Gain insight and understanding on where you are and map out a good strategy to get to where you are headed. Use what you do not like to build and recreate a better you.

Reframe Your Experiences for A Better Mental and Emotional Picture

The outer area is the frame containing your thoughts, emotions and responses.

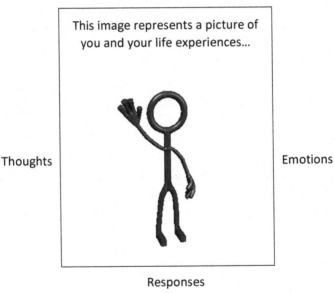

The way you view your life experiences is determined by how you frame those experiences through thoughts, emotions, and responses. Today you can begin to reframe with positivity.

Picture This...

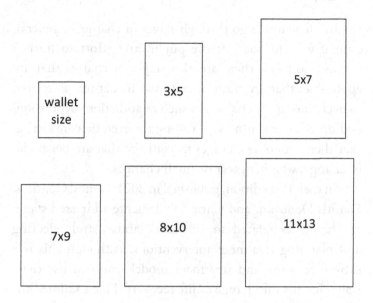

Each frame represents your mind, and the numbers represent the measurement of your thought processes. As you have learned new insights the number increases and the frame enlarges. Perhaps you were once a wallet size thinker, but now you have matured and developed into a greater mindset of a 7 X 9 thinker. If you try to revert back to wallet size thinking you will not fit into that old frame. Your thinking has enlarged. Therefore, to fit back into a smaller frame you would have to reduce your thinking and mentality.

Stages of Change

In life you will go through stages of change in general, even if you do not actually put in any effort to initiate change; however, there are also stages of change that are applicable, that are more intentional in nature, as related to overcoming life challenges such as addiction, depression, and other mental illnesses. You might even be considering that there are some changes in your life that are beneficial to change, whether great or small changes.

In their first edition, published in 2001, Gerard Connors, Dennis Donovan, and Carlo DiClemente addressed stages of change as related to substance abuse, and selecting and planning treatment interventions. Although this is a substance abuse and treatment model, you can use these stages for any life change or life recovery. I have tailored the stages to be more generalized to any change, and not just substance issues. You see, these stages are applicable in any situation in life when you are considering change.

The stages I will present are extracted from the following 5 stages of change:

Pre-contemplation, Contemplation, Preparation, Action, and Maintenance.

Pre-contemplation

In Stage 1 of change is the idea that you are not thinking about change because you have not yet determined a need for change. Although others might have pointed out some things about your choices, attitude, and behaviors that are concerning. You will remain at the pre-contemplation stage until you see the need for a change. I want you to think about your life as you ponder what this stage of change means. As you reflect and introspect, do you see any area of your life that is stifled, unfulfilling, perhaps you have grown stale or bored with certain aspects of *you*. Let me remind you, the issue can be something great or small, but consider if making any change at all is in your best interest.

Oftentimes, imagining a need for change is difficult because you might have a high tolerance for putting up with certain things. Also, there are times when individuals are in a dynamic with self and/or others for so long, that it seems things should just be the way they have always been, and/or there is a loss of hope that change is possible, or that any efforts will make a difference at all. Another reason you might get stuck in pre-contemplation is if you think others need to change, and the problem is not you.

Keep in mind, you are responsible for you. So, even if the issue is with others and you are in a problematic relationship with such persons, you might consider incorporating more healthy relationships in your life. However, I always say this and I stand by this saying: you do not have a problem until you call it a problem. Identifying problems that need to change is the first step to getting to work on Stage 2: Contemplation.

Contemplation

In this stage the intent to change is present. This means that there is awareness of change that is necessary. At this juncture, the benefits of change are at the forefront of your mind. Nevertheless, you are keenly aware of the costs of making changes. During this stage you are imaging the differences you would like to see, or perhaps the possibilities that life can be different…better. So, soliloquize or talk it over with yourself, not in a filibustering kind of way that could delay necessary action.

Some of my patients have asked if there is something wrong with talking to yourself. I honestly cannot think of anyone better than myself to talk to. Of course, the goal is to confer with yourself to understand and decide better, and not to get caught up in neurotic replaying of events that does not lead to a productive end.

It is at this point of contemplation that you are giving consideration of the person you will morph into and how empowering it will be for you to finally be in control of your thoughts and emotions. You understand that the process of change will not be easy, but you are definitely thinking the change is worth it. More and more you think: the benefits you will experience are more important, and keeping a firm mindset will help you when the challenges of what change costs seems to overtake you. With this thought in mind, you are poised for Stage 3: Preparation.

Preparation

Stage 3, the preparation stage, is when you actually engage in planning and fine-tuning your plans. During this stage you are most likely to depend on literature relevant to your goals. You might also find that you are, more and more, surrounding yourself with likeminded individuals. Your language begins to change to reflect that you are truly ready to take on this opportunity to implement your desired changes.

Additionally, you might notice you are more interested in what it means to be self-aware, to understand how you are hard-wired, and to get in touch with your particular proclivities that impede your ability to be your best *you*. In tandem with implementing stages of change, you might seek out partnership with a professional counselor, life coach, or spiritual advisor. You are in the preparation stage, you understand what is required, and now your mind is set and ready for Stage 4: Action.

Action

In this stage of change you are actually practicing new ways of thinking and responding to yourself, people, life, and the world. Already, you are able to see your goals taking shape and form in accordance to what you desire. You are making healthier choices, learning to think before you respond, and you are becoming more astute at problem-solving and conflict resolution.

Now that you are able to experience a stronger, more confident *you*, you want more of the same. You are stoked and pumped about gaining more insights and you actually look forward to opportunities to try out your newly discovered ways of engaging and interacting. Your depression has lifted, you feel a sense of life satisfaction, and you want more of the same continually. Now you are ready for Stage 5: Maintenance.

Maintenance

This final stage of change is the stage where you experience sustained progress. Yep, you are feeling pretty good about what you have accomplished. You are being commended by others who notice the new you. You also feel the satisfaction of your new trajectory and what it means for your communication, relationships, emotions, and overall mood. Perhaps the old you experienced tantrums, you were short-fused, edgy, and angry; maybe in your anger you would hit, throw and break things. If that does not describe you maybe this does: maybe you used to find it hard to be light-hearted or laugh, or perhaps you used to be passive -aggressive; but today you are different. Today you are enjoying the simplicity of life along with the seriousness of life, but in balance. You are not just one-dimensional. You are no longer bound by issues that are depressing; therefore, you feel light, and liberated.

However, do not be surprised that there will be times in life when an event happens or an issue arises that you are not quite prepared for, and you might regress in your response. Do not allow this to cause you to forget how far you have come. Life can happen to even the strongest person who is usually good at coping, but no one is on their A game all the time. You cannot know how you might spontaneously respond when life throws you a curve ball. But be assured, you now know things that you cannot unknow, and getting back on course is what you now know.

So, if you end up in a place in life that is hard and you feel things are becoming unmanageable, go back to the drawing board. Go back to the resources that were a source of strength for you: get back to your literature, journal writing, counseling, meditation, and so on. Whatever worked before, just rework it. You do not have to stew in a stuck place ever again.

This example comes to mind. I love the way analogies can work, so I will share. If you have ever stewed a chicken before you would definitely relate, but if not, here's new information for you. It really does matter if you have quality cookware, because chicken tends to stick, especially if overcooked or not cooked properly. Having quality cookware might not necessarily prevent sticking when cooking chicken, especially if cooking chicken with the skin on. Stay with me, there is a point to this example. It is definitely easier to clean quality cookware and deal with stuck-on food more effectively. Tough stewed chicken issues cannot stand up to quality cookware, the material that quality cookware is made up of is durable. Quality cookware is built and designed to sustain cooking challenges

Here is the point for your life of stuckness. You know too much now. You have too much strength and power now. You are of a better quality in your communication, emotion management, problem-solving, decision-making and so on. You are much like the quality cookware, you are durable. Life cannot stand up to your current strength and leave you in a stuck place. Sure, life will be difficult, like the stuck-on chicken I described, but the new you will be able to let it wash off much more efficiently than before you made significant changes. You can recover and continue to practice what you have learned during *your* stages of change.

Anti-depression Meal

1 ounce of reflection
1 cup of meditation
1 side of quietness
1 slice of solitude
1 tallest glass of refreshing drink of peace of mind

This is the one meal that you cannot get too much of. Feast and drink as much as you can stand. The only thing that can present as somewhat of a kibosh or thwart regarding your plan to implement this meal to your daily diet intake, is your lack of discipline. Only you can make this a priority. The level of your investment can reveal the level of your discomfort to begin implementing these qualities. What I mean by this is: boundaries will be necessary and some people in your relationship circle might not understand or even care that you need to incorporate these factors in your lifestyle, and this might influence you; additionally, your own stubbornness, fatigue, and/or lack of discipline might get in the way from time-to-time.

So, if you demonstrate low-level of investment, this might be grist for the mill in understanding that the challenge is quite challenging for you. Not only can the level of your investment indicate the level of your discomfort, the level of your investment will also determine your outcome—no pain, no gain! Know your strengths, know your limitations, be patient during the process.

Self-Care

Self-care is identified as the ability to balance between emotional and physical stressors. When you fail to manage stress effectively, you deal with what is called burnout. Burnout can lead to depression if left unattended. Some signs of burnout are:

Exhaustion and lack of motivation: cognitive issues, having your mind scattered in many different directions all at once. Difficulty leaving work at work. Being overly concerned and invested in things that are out of your control.

Lack of self-care and decrease life satisfaction: not focusing on good sleep hygiene. Not focusing on healthy eating. Not focusing on proper exercise. Not focusing on unrealized passions and life goals. Job performance or school performance problems. Low morale in the workplace, lackadaisical attitude toward work and school, when at one time you were more responsible.

Interpersonal difficulties, frequent conflict and arguments: arguing more with spouse or significant other, low tolerance level with your children, not able to manage communication and relationships in a healthy manner. Short-fused, edgy, easily set off, overly critical, and negative. Cynical and jaded. Focusing on what is not working, pessimistic and doubtful that things can improve.

Precursors to burnout

- Lack of effective boundaries, difficulty saying no. Inability to say no can stem from various encounters. The purpose of spotlighting this point is to elicit awareness about the awkwardness some individuals experience as related to the word "no," and also to encourage you to begin erecting healthy, flexible boundaries. Difficulty setting healthy boundaries can lead to depression, in that; always being available and expending yourself can lead to stress, burnout, and ultimately depression. There are many resources and self-help material to aid in this process (some are located in the recommended reading section of this book), and of course therapy or counseling can help.

- Perfectionism. Being a perfectionist has its perks; however, being a perfectionist can also lead to depression. Perfectionists tend to be turned on the on position mostly and getting adequate sleep and much needed down time is generally not experienced by perfectionists. Other medical issues can also be experienced by perfectionists who do not have a shut-off valve. Associated with the perfectionist's attitude or mindset is the idea that good enough is never really good enough.

When I work with perfectionistic patients, one of my goals is to highlight the reality that perfectionists do not tend to have a ceiling. Here is what I mean, although a ceiling of good-enough is set by the perfectionist, when the time comes that the ceiling is reached, simultaneously the ceiling is raised by perfectionists who are never really satisfied with standards they set for themselves. This dynamic could not only lead to depression, but anxiety as well.

• Workaholics. If you find that you are a workaholic, you might resonate with the worker who rarely takes a break. By this I mean that you eat lunch at your desk, and you do not take time to step away and enjoy the lunch break you have earned. Remember, you are not being paid extra for not taking lunch; of course, if it is approved by your boss—I guess. I remember when I was employed by someone else, not taking lunch was on me. You snooze it you lose it.

Another sign of being a workaholic is when you take work home, when you find it difficult to stop thinking about work when you are away from work. There is no real reward for neglecting your needs. Unless, you live alone; someone is expecting you to be "all" there when you arrive home. Even if there is only a pet at home, be "all" there with the pet. If you are the only one home, pay respect to your unique needs and the downtime you deserve after giving your time to work most of the day. Sooner or later you will encounter stress, and subsequently burnout; and possibly depression if you do not deal with a workaholic mindset.

One way to mitigate the possibility of sliding down the slippery slope of too-loose or no boundaries, perfectionism, and being a workaholic is to think healthy. In this book there are many ways to establish and maintain a holistic healthy lifestyle, and do not forget the power of play, as it relates to your overall health, vitality, and life satisfaction. Sometimes people forget the value of play, especially adults. And unfortunately, some people play too much and do not know how to take life seriously as needed. Choose to stay balanced and this choice can serve you well.

When you do not deal with stress appropriately, you begin to lose some things.

Take note and be careful not to allow yourself to ignore stress. You can possibly avoid burnout that could ultimately lead to feeling depressed.

Conclusion

As our time together has come to an end I trust that you have garnered necessary insights and tools, and you are equipped with understanding and strategies to get you through times of difficulty and challenges. For sure, life will always do what life always does. Life challenges you, I know; sometimes to the very core and fiber of all you might have counted on within yourself. But do not doubt just because life is overwhelming. Life will be easier at times, but not so easy at other times. All-in-all, you have what it takes. You now have additional information to aid you as you continue your life's journey. You will continue to build and perfect your coping and ability to overcome when life issues would otherwise hold you down.

I am aware that you might not resonate with everything presented in this reading. My suggestion: go through this material as with a "fine-tooth comb." Your take away will be whatever you resonate with. You will discover what you need and it will be useful for you. Much like eating fish. There are times when bones still remain in fish when you eat it. Generally, you would not eat fish bones. Therefore, you eat the meat and you discard the bones. Likewise, perhaps not all insights, principles, and strategies in this book will be what you need or find helpful; but I am confident your time indulging will be well spent.

My goal is that you are now more aware of and able to recognize, more astutely, the signs, and different types of depression, implications of depressions, as well as treatment options. It is also my desire that with understanding of a sunken place, you are now armed and equipped to recognize and address those dark moments in life more effectively. Finally, I trust that you have enjoyed the personal testimony and encouragement of Justin's story, and that you will apply principle's you have gleaned from chapter 8: Let's Talk about Healthy. Take these nuggets and kernels of knowledge into your everyday, and share with others in word and in action, exactly how you can laugh again.

I am confident that you will hold dear and utilize the knowledge and resources in this reading material and these principles will continue to resoundingly ring in your heart and mind; holding you together so that you will not fall apart and sink to that sunken place that depression prepares for you. The battle will always remain between your two ears and in your heart, impacting your mind and your emotions, but have no fear. You possess the power of mind to overcome. Perception and perspective both matter, and both of these qualities can determine the difference in your response. As I stated earlier, you will always be challenged, but you will get through and *win*.

Below, I have composed encouragement that I believe will be a source of comfort for you. As you read just know that you are much stronger than you realize at times, and sure, there are times of weakness. Be patient with, and gracious to yourself. After all, when everything is said and done, just know that your higher *self* will kick in and come to the rescue when you feel weak and defeated.

Dear depression…So long!

I did not recognize you when you entered my life, All I knew was that you came along with great pain and strife. Before I knew it, I was caught in your grip, and slowly but surely my life you did strip. You invaded my peace and left me at a place of dis-ease. You tore down my self-esteem and shattered my hopes and my dreams. You left me dry, cracked, and drained, and my self-confidence was greatly stained. I felt so much dread, as you played games with my head; somehow all along I knew you wanted me dead. I could not win no matter how hard I fought; you sold me lies, and your lies I bought. But then one day I discovered something about you, you are not able to do anything that I don't allow you to do. Sure, you are very real and a strong force to defeat, but the moment I realized my strength and self-worth, I also realized that depression can be beat. It might be tough and require a lot of effort and will, but you will be long gone and I will still be right here, standing still. My life will shine once again and I will soar, because I refuse to allow you to control me anymore. You see, you are a part of my experiences and the way that I think, but I am rising now, I won't continue to sink. I won't sink further into that sunken place that you have prepared for me. Today and for the rest of my life I am forever free. So long depression:

You are done and I've finally won!

RECOMMENDED READING

American Foundaton of Suicidal Prevention. www.afsp.org. (800) 273-TALK or 8255.

Bechtle, M. (2012). People Can't Drive You Crazy If You Don't Give Them The Keys. Baker Publishing Group. Grand Rapids, MI.

Bechtle, M. (2016). I wish I Had Come With Instructions: the woman's guide to a man's brain. Revell Publishing. Grand Rapids, MI.

Chodron, P. (1997). When Things Fall Apart: heart advice for difficult times. Shambhala Publications. Boston, MA.

Cloud, H., Ph.D. & Townsend, J., Ph.D. (1992). Boundaries: when to say yes when to say no to take control of your life. Zondervan. Grand Rapids, MI.

Crabb, L. (1997). Connecting: healing for ourselves and our relationships. World Publishing. Nashville, TN.

Crabb, L. (1999). The Safest Place On Earth: where people connect and are forever changed. World Publishing. Nashville, TN.

De Choudhury, M., Gamon, M., Counts, S., & Horvitz, E. (2013). Predicting Depression via Social Media. Microsoft Research Redmond, WA. (www.aaai.org).

Gordon, J. (2007). The Energy Bus. John Wiley and Sons, Inc. Hoboken, New Jersey.

Gordon, J. (2012). The Positive Dog. John Wiley and Sons, Inc. Hoboken, New Jersey

Harry Mill, PhD., Natalie Reiss, PhD., and Mark Dombeck, PhD. Socialization and Altruistic Acts as Stress Relief. Mentalhelp.net, 2008. https://www.mentalhelp.net/articles/socialization-and-altruistic-acts-as-stress-relief/

Hidaka, B.H. B.A. MD/PhD Candidate. (2012). Depression as a Disease of Modernity: explanations for increasing prevalence. https://www.ncbi.nim.nih.gov/pms/articles/PMC3330161/

Twenge, J., Gentile, B., DeWall, C., Ma D, Lacefield K., Schurtz, D. Birth Cohort Increases In Psychopathology Among Young Americans. Clinical Psychology Review. 2010; 30: 145-154.

ABOUT THE AUTHOR

Crystal Scott-Lindsey is a Licensed Marriage and Family Therapist in the states of California, Texas, and Michigan. She holds a Master's Degree in Counseling Psychology as well as a certificate in Pastoral Counseling from Holy Names University, Oakland, CA. Crystal graduated Magna cum Laude with a Bachelor's of Science Degree in Organizational Management from Patten University, Oakland CA. Her primary private practice location is in the DFW Texas Region, which she established over 5 years ago after relocating from the California, San Francisco Bay Area. Crystal opened her second private practice location in Detroit Michigan 2 years ago. She has been in her role as therapist for more than 14 years. Her credentials afford her opportunities to provide critical incident and stress debriefing (CISD) services to many organizations and employment companies. Crystal also facilitates teaching and training on various topics for mental health, coping, and employee assistance needs. Additionally, Crystal is the author of *Take Back Your Life, Sin and the Church, and Communication and You.*

NOTES

NOTES

NOTES

NOTES

NOTES

NOTES